HOW **NOT TO** **KILL** YOUR HOUSEPLANT

Penguin
Random
House

Editor Toby Mann

Senior Art Editor Alison Gardner

Designers Rehan Abdul, Karen Constanti

Editorial assistance
Alice Horne, Tia Sarkar

Jacket Designer Steven Marsden

Jacket Co-ordinator Laura Bithell

Pre-production Producer Robert Dunn

Print Producer Ché Creasey

Creative Technical Support
Sonia Charbonnier

Managing Editor Dawn Henderson

Managing Art Editor
Marianne Markham

Art Director Maxine Pedliham

Publishing Director Mary-Clare Jerram

Illustrations Debbie Maizels

Photography Will Heap

First published in
Great Britain in 2017 by

Dorling Kindersley Limited,
80 Strand, London WC2R ORL

Copyright © 2017
Dorling Kindersley Limited
A Penguin Random House Company

8 10 9
027–305974–Mar/17

A CIP catalogue record for this book
is available from the British Library.
ISBN: 978-0-2413-0217-0

Printed and bound in China

A WORLD OF IDEAS:
SEE ALL THERE IS TO KNOW

www.dk.com

HOW **NOT TO** KILL YOUR HOUSEPLANT

Survival tips for the HORTICULTURALLY CHALLENGED

Veronica Peerless

CONTENTS

With specific care details for 119 different plants, this section provides all the information you need to treasure your houseplant and troubleshoot any problems.

Top 5 plants for:

FIND YOUR PLANT

URN PLANT
Aechmea fasciata
pp.34–35

MAIDENHAIR FERN
Adiantum raddianum
pp.32–33

FLAMING SWORD
Vriesea splendens
p.35

CRETAN BRAKE FERN
Pteris cretica
p.33

GUZMANIA
Guzmania lingulata
p.35

HARE'S FOOT FERN
Davillia canariensis
p.33

ELEPHANT'S EAR
Alocasia x amazonica
pp.36–37

ALOE VERA
Aloe vera
pp. 38–39

EMERALD FERN
Asparagus densiflorus
Sprengeri Group
pp. 42–43

ELIATOR HYBRIDS
Begonia Eliator Group
p. 45

BLUSHING BROMELIAD
Neoregelia carolinae
f. tricolor
p. 49

AGAVE
Agave
p. 39

ASPARAGUS FERN
Asparagus setaceus
p. 43

TUBEROUS BEGONIAS
Begonia spp.
p. 45

PEACOCK PLANT
Calathea
pp. 50–51

HAWORTHIA
Haworthia
p. 39

SHAMROCK PLANT
Oxalis triangularis
p. 43

QUEEN'S TEARS
Billbergia nutans
pp. 48–49

PRAYER PLANT
Maranta
p. 51

FLAMINGO FLOWER
Anthurium
pp. 40–41

PAINTED-LEAF BEGONIA
Begonia rex
pp. 44–45

PINK QUILL
Tillandsia cyanea
p. 49

STROMANTHE
Stromanthe
p. 51

continued

SPIDER PLANT
Chlorophytum comosum
pp. 52–53

MINIATURE ROSES
Rosa
p. 55

STRING OF BEADS
Senecio rowleyanus
p. 59

DUMB CANE
Dieffenbachia
pp. 62–63

POTHOS
Epipremnum
p. 53

PRIMROSE
Primula vulgaris
p. 55

HEARTS ON A STRING
Ceropegia woodii
p. 59

**HEART-LEAF
PHILODENDRON**
Philodendron scandens
p. 63

ARROWHEAD PLANT
Syngonium podophyllum
p. 53

NATAL LILY
Clivia miniata
pp. 56–57

FLORISTS' CYCLAMEN
Cyclamen persicum
pp. 60–61

**BLUSHING
PHILODENDRON**
Philodendron erubescens
p. 63

POT MUM
Chrysanthemum
pp. 54–55

MONEY PLANT
Crassula ovata
pp. 58–59

INDIAN AZALEA
Rhododendron simsii
p. 61

VENUS FLY TRAP
Dionaea muscipula
pp. 64–65

PITCHER PLANT
Sarracenia
p.65

SONG OF INDIA
Dracaena reflexa
p.69

TIGER JAWS
Faucaria
p.73

RUBBER PLANT
Ficus elastica
p.77

MONKEY CUPS
Nepenthes
p.65

LUCKY BAMBOO
Dracaena sanderiana
pp.70–71

POINSETTIA
Euphorbia pulcherrima
pp.74–75

NERVE PLANT
Fittonia
pp.78–79

DRAGON TREE
Dracaena fragrans
pp.68–69

HEN & CHICKS
Echeveria
p.72–73

FIDDLE-LEAF FIG
Ficus lyrata
pp.76–77

VELVET PLANT
Gynura aurantiaca
p.79

**MADAGASCAR
DRAGON TREE**
Dracaena marginata
p.69

AEONIUM
Aeonium
p.73

WEEPING FIG
Ficus benjamina
p.77

POLKA DOT PLANT
Hypoestes
p.79

continued

ENGLISH IVY
Hedera helix
pp. 80–81

KENTIA PALM
Howea fosteriana
pp. 84–85

MINIATURE WAX PLANT
Hoya bella
p. 89

SWISS CHEESE PLANT
Monstera deliciosa
pp. 94-95

SPOTTED LAUREL
Aucuba japonica
p. 81

PARLOUR PALM
Chamaedorea elegans
p. 85

FLAMING KATY
Kalanchoe blossfeldiana
pp. 90–91

**HORSEHEAD
PHILODENDRON**
*Philodendron
bipinnatifidum*
p. 95

JAPANESE ARALIA
Fatsia japonica
p. 81

BUTTERFLY PALM
Dypsis lutescens
p. 85

CALANDIVA
Kalanchoe
Calandiva® Series
p. 91

SWISS CHEESE VINE
Monstera obliqua
p. 95

AMARYLLIS
Hippeastrum
pp. 82–83

INDIAN ROPE PLANT
Hoya carnosa
pp. 88–89

SENSITIVE PLANT
Mimosa pudica
pp. 92–93

BOSTON FERN
Nephrolepis exaltata
'Bostoniensis'
pp. 96–97

BIRD'S NEST FERN
Asplenium nidus
p.97

CROWN CACTUS
Rebutia
p.99

MOTH ORCHID
Phalaenopsis
pp.102–103

MISSIONARY PLANT
Pilea peperomioides
pp.108–109

SILVER LADY
Blechnum gibbum
p.97

RADIATOR PLANT
Peperomia metallica
pp.100–101

PYGMY DATE PALM
Phoenix roebelenii
pp.104–105

FRIENDSHIP PLANT
Pilea involucrata
'Moon Valley'
p.109

DESERT CACTI
Opuntia
pp.98–99

CREEPING BUTTONS
Peperomia rotundifolia
p.101

LADY PALM
Rhapsis excelsa
p.105

ALUMINIUM PLANT
Pilea cadierei
p.109

MONK'S HOOD
Astrophytum ornatum
p.99

BABY RUBBER PLANT
Peperomia obtusifolia
p.101

DWARF FAN PALM
Chamaerops humilis
p.105

STAGHORN FERN
Platycerium bifurcatum
pp.110–111

continued

REGAL ELKHORN FERN
Platycerium grande
p.111

AFRICAN MILK BUSH
Euphorbia trigona
p.115

CROTON
Codiaeum variegatum
p.119

MISTLETOE CACTUS
Rhipsalis baccifera
p.121

AFRICAN VIOLET
Saintpaulia
pp.112–113

CREEPING SAXIFRAGE
Saxifraga stolonifera
pp.116–117

ZEBRA PLANT
Aphelandra squarrosa
p.119

BABY'S TEARS
Soleirolia soleirolii
pp.122–123

SNAKE PLANT
Sansevieria trifasciata
pp.114–115

SWEDISH IVY
Plectranthus
p.117

CHRISTMAS CACTUS
Schlumbergera buckleyi
pp.120–121

PIGGYBACK PLANT
Tolmiea menziesii
p.123

AFRICAN SPEAR
Sansevieria cylindrica
p.115

UMBRELLA TREE
Schefflera arboricola
pp.118–119

EASTER CACTUS
Schlumbergera gaetneri
p.121

BEAD PLANT
Nertera granadensis
p.123

PEACE LILY
Spathiphyllum
pp.124–125

CAPE PRIMROSE
Streptocarpus
pp.130–131

FLAME NETTLE
Solenostemon
p.135

ZZ PLANT
Zamioculcas zamiifolia
pp.138–139

CHINESE EVERGREEN
Aglaonema
p.125

GLOXINIA
Sinningia speciosa
p.131

YUCCA
Yucca elephantipes
pp.136–137

SAGO PALM
Cycas revoluta
p.139

CAST IRON PLANT
Aspidistra eliator
p.125

AIR PLANTS
Tillandsia
pp.132–133

CABBAGE PALM
Cordyline australis
p.137

GUINEA CHESTNUT
Pachira aquatica
p.139

BIRD OF PARADISE
Strelitzia reginae
pp.128–129

INCH PLANT
Tradescantia zebrina
pp.134–135

PONYTAIL PALM
Beaucarnea recurvata
p.137

INDOOR BONSAI
Various
pp.140–142

THE **BASICS**

What every
houseplant needs
to stay alive

BUY IT

If possible, buy your houseplant from a nursery or garden centre, where it will have been properly cared for. Here are a few things to consider when choosing a houseplant, including how to get it home without killing it!

SHAPE

Ensure that the plant has a good shape. Look for bushy plants, and avoid those that are leggy or spindly.

Dumb cane
(pp.62–63)

COMPOST

Test the compost to see if it's moist. It shouldn't be soggy or very dry, as these are signs that the plant may not have been watered properly.

ROOTS

If there are lots of roots visible on top of the compost and underneath the bottom of the pot, the plant is pot-bound (or root-bound). Avoid these plants as they will have been struggling to thrive and so won't be in peak condition.

FLOWERING PLANTS

When choosing a flowering plant, make sure it has both flowers and buds. Plants with buds will last longer as these buds will open and replace older, fading flowers. Avoid plants with only tightly closed buds, as these may not open when you get the plant home.

Pot mum (pp.54–55)

WRAP IT UP

Spring or summer is the best time to buy a houseplant, as the weather is often milder and the plant won't be too "shocked" by the sudden change in temperature and location. If you are buying a plant in winter when it is cold, be sure to wrap it up when taking it home, as the sudden change in temperature can cause the buds or leaves to fall off some plants, or even kill others. Poinsettias are particularly vulnerable to the cold.

CONDITION

Check that the leaves are fresh and have a good colour, with no signs of browning or yellowing.

PESTS & DISEASES

Look for signs of pests or diseases, making sure to check the undersides of the leaves (see Plant pests, pp.24–27, and Plant diseases, pp.28–29).

Poinsettia (pp.74–75)

POT IT & PLACE IT

Once you get your houseplant home, you'll need to check your plant is in a pot with drainage holes, and find a suitable location for it. Doing these two things will go a long way towards helping you keep it healthy.

HOW TO POT IT...

Most houseplants come in plastic pots with drainage holes in the bottom. You can put these inside more ornamental pots. Some plants are sold in ornamental pots with no drainage holes. This makes it difficult to judge whether water is gathering at the bottom of the pot and rotting the roots. It's best to repot these plants into a plastic pot with drainage holes – this could be a plastic pot that you hide within a more attractive one.

Dumb cane (pp.62–63)

Ensure the plastic pot fits into the pot you want to use

Drainage holes

PLANTS SOLD IN PLASTIC POTS
Check to see if your plant is in a pot with drainage holes at the bottom.

REPOTTING INTO A PLASTIC POT
If your plant is sold in only an ornamental pot, repot it into a plastic pot with drainage holes before concealing it in an ornamental container.

WHERE TO PUT IT...

To find the right spot for your plant, think about temperature, light, and humidity. Consider your plant's natural habitat – plants native to the rainforest floor won't enjoy a sun-baked windowsill. Check your plant's needs and put it in a place that suits it, not you.

LIGHT

Light is a houseplant's source of energy, and some plants need more light than others. Most houseplants do well in bright, indirect or filtered light, out of direct sunlight. They are usually best placed around 1m (3ft) away from a north-, east-, or west-facing window. Bear in mind that the light can change during the course of the day, and at different times of year.

Aloe vera (pp.38–39)

TEMPERATURE

Most houseplants enjoy the same conditions we do – warm during the day, and cooler at night. Some plants, such as ivy and cyclamen, prefer lower temperatures. Houseplants do not enjoy significant fluctuations in temperature, so avoid the following places:

→ Near a radiator
→ Near an air-conditioning unit
→ In draughts
→ On a windowsill, behind curtains at night

You could use a thermometer to check room temperature

HUMIDITY

Most houseplants need more humidity than is available in the average, centrally heated home, but some rooms, such as bathrooms and kitchens, are more humid than others. To create humidity, fill a tray or dish that is the same width as the plant with pebbles or gravel. Pour in water, keeping the level at just below the top of the pebbles. Then place your plant on top. The water will produce humidity as it evaporates. Alternatively, mist the leaves of your plant using a hand mister. Mist in the morning, so the leaves dry before night. How often your plant needs misting depends on the room. Look for signs that your plant needs humidity, such as brown leaf tips, increasing how often you mist if they occur. Use distilled, filtered, or rainwater if your area has hard water. Grouping plants together will also increase humidity.

Boston fern (pp.96–97)

Parlour palm (p.85)   **Kentia palm (pp.84–85)**

WATER IT

Incorrect watering is the main reason that houseplants die – particularly overwatering. Here are the best methods to water healthy plants and save wilted ones.

||||||||||||||||||||||||||||||||||||||||||||||||||||||||||||||||||||

HOW TO WATER IT...

Most plants can be watered from above. If your plant has hairy leaves, however, or the foliage covers the compost, water it from below to avoid splashing the leaves. Orchids can be dipped and drained – it allows their coarse compost to absorb the right amount of water. Water your plants with tepid water so that the water temperature doesn't shock them. It's also worth leaving a bucket outside (if possible) to collect rainwater. Some plants, such as bromeliads, prefer it, as they are sensitive to the chemicals in hard tap water.

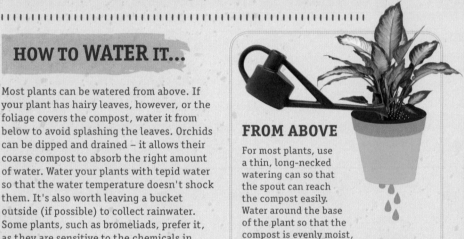

FROM ABOVE

For most plants, use a thin, long-necked watering can so that the spout can reach the compost easily. Water around the base of the plant so that the compost is evenly moist, and allow the excess water to drain away.

Dumb cane (pp.62–63)

FROM BELOW

Use this method to avoid splashing the leaves, which will create ugly marks and lead to the leaves rotting. Stand the pot in a saucer of water for around 30 minutes. Drain any excess water from the saucer.

Cyclamen (pp.60–61)

DIP & DRAIN

A good technique for watering orchids – place the pot in a container of tepid water and leave it to stand for around 10 minutes. Let it drain thoroughly.

Moth orchid (pp.102–103)

HOW MUCH WATER...

Here are some things to consider when working out whether your plant needs watering, and how much water to give it.

→ **Overwatering** is the number one cause of houseplant death. But be sure not to underwater either.

→ **Don't water to a timetable** – get to know your plant's needs instead. Most plants only need watering when the top 1-2cm (½–¾in) of compost is dry – gently poke your finger into the soil to test it. If a rosette of leaves is covering the compost, go by the weight of the pot – a very light pot will have dry compost.

→ **Aim to make the compost moist**, but not wet. Most houseplants hate sitting in soggy compost, so always let excess water drain away.

→ **Compost in terracotta pots dries out more quickly** than that in plastic or ceramic pots, this is because terracotta is a porous material.

→ **Most plants need less water in winter** as they are not actively growing. Some plants need this period of winter rest to reflower.

WILTING DUE TO UNDERWATERING?

If your plant has wilted, it may be due to a lack of water. Check that the compost is dry to ensure that your plant has been underwatered, as overwatering can have the same effect.

☀ **SAVE IT** *Move your plant somewhere shady and fill a bowl with tepid water. In just its plastic pot with drainage holes, dunk your plant into the water, weighing it down if it floats. Soak for around 30 minutes and drain. The plant should revive within an hour.*

Peace lily (pp.124–125)

WILTING DUE TO OVERWATERING?

Plants can also wilt due to waterlogging. This is much more serious as it can kill your plant more quickly than underwatering.

❤ **SAVE IT** *Remove your plant from its pot(s) and wrap the root ball with newspaper or paper towels, replacing them until they have soaked up all the moisture. Repot the plant into fresh compost and keep the plant out of direct sun. Keep the compost just moist for a few weeks.*

Remove your plant from both its pots

African violet (pp.112–113)

FEED IT & LOVE IT

You need to do more than just water your plant to keep it alive – most plants need feeding too. It's also worth spending a few minutes each week examining and grooming your plant – it will thrive on your attention.

FEEDING

All plants need food to thrive. Carnivorous plants capture prey to feed on, but most houseplants will need to be fed. You should start feeding your plant a few weeks after you get it home, or around a couple of months after it has been repotted. In spring and summer, add a liquid houseplant feed to your watering can – usually around once a month. Be sure to follow the manufacturer's instructions and don't be tempted to add extra – overfeeding can damage the plant. It's best to feed when the compost is already moist – that way it will reach the roots directly and won't drain away. Alternatively, add slow-release pellets or spikes to the compost as a more low-maintenance approach – they'll release a little food every time you water. Don't feed houseplants in winter, unless they are winter-flowering.

Umbrella tree (pp.118–119)

Add liquid feed to the water

Add fertilizer pellets to the compost

EXTRA CARE

Get to know your plant by spending a minute or two every week examining it and making sure it looks good. This is not only an important way to keep it healthy, but will mean you'll spot signs of problems more quickly when they occur.

GROOMING

Remove old leaves and deadhead flowers – this will encourage more blooms and will prevent dead petals from landing on the foliage, causing it to rot.

CLEANING

Wipe your plant's leaves (especially those with large leaves) with a clean, damp cloth to keep them dust-free, as dust can prevent light getting to the leaves. Stand palms in a a tepid shower in winter, or a rain shower in summer. Furry-leaved or prickly plants are best cleaned with a soft paintbrush.

Remove old, brown leaves

Dragon tree (pp.68–69)

Use a paintbrush for furry leaves

Use a damp cloth to wipe waxy leaves

INSPECTING

Prevention is better than cure. If you notice that your plant is looking sickly, check your care regime and look for signs of pests or diseases before they have a chance to cause significant problems (see Plant pests, pp.24–27, & Plant diseases, pp.28–29).

Whitefly

Aphids

REPOT IT

Sooner or later, your plant's original compost will be exhausted, so your plant will need repotting. Chances are that the plant will have grown, too, so the plant will need "potting on" into a slightly larger pot.

WHEN TO POT ON

Most plants need potting on when their roots are curling around the edge of the compost; carefully remove the root ball to check. When repotting, choose a pot that's only slightly larger than the previous one – an extra 5cm (2in) in diameter is about right. A much larger pot will house too much compost and get waterlogged. Most plants are happy in multi-purpose or indoor plant compost, but some need a specialist mix, such as orchids and cacti. Do not use garden soil. The best time to pot on is spring or summer. Some plants can look a little unhappy shortly after repotting, but they should recover – just continue to care for them as normal.

Fresh compost

PLANTS IN SMALLER POTS

Repot smaller plants into a new, larger pot, with fresh compost.

Roots coming out of the bottom of the plant pot

Dumb cane (pp.62–63)

PLANTS IN LARGE POTS

It can be hard to take large, mature plants out of their containers, so "top dress" them instead. Remove the top 5–8cm (2–3in) of compost with a small trowel or spoon (take care not to damage roots) and replace it with fresh.

Fiddle-leaf fig (pp.76–77)

HOW TO POT ON

Follow the steps to pot on your plant correctly. You will need a new pot and fresh compost.

1 Water your plant the day before you repot it. It will be easier to remove and less likely to be "shocked" by repotting.

2 Add fresh compost to the base of the new slightly larger pot.

3 Holding your plant upside down around the base of the stems, tap it out of its pot.

6 Water your plant, allowing any excess to drain away.

Leave 2–3cm (1in) at the top of the pot

4 Sit your plant in the new pot. Leave space between the surface of the compost and the top of the pot.

5 Add compost around the root ball, firming it in gently.

"After repotting your plant, continue to care for it as normal."

PLANT PESTS

Houseplants can be troubled by small unwelcome guests that can damage and even kill them. Here's how to identify the signs of a pest infestation, and what you can do to save your plant.

HOW TO STOP PESTS

The best way to avoid pests is to keep your plant healthy – pests are more likely to attack stressed, unhealthy plants.

If your plant does become infested with a pest, in many cases you will be able to treat it with an insecticide, either chemical or natural. Natural products are derived from plants or other natural substances.

Sticky traps are especially good for trapping aphids, whitefly, and thrips, and can help you monitor the level of infestation.

If you have a lot of houseplants in one place that are all suffering from the same problem, you could try a biological control. These natural products are available by mail order and work by introducing predators (usually invisible to the naked eye) to attack the pests.

Sticky trap

Begonia (pp.44–45)

Key
Where you will find the pests on your plants

Buds & stems | On the leaves | In the soil

"Pests are more likely to attack stressed, unhealthy plants."

THE PESTS

You may find signs of these pests on your houseplants. Plants that are particularly prone to infestation will have more details on their care page.

WHITEFLIES

They hide on the undersides of leaves, and clouds of tiny white insects will fly up when your plant is disturbed.

❤️ TREAT IT *Take your plant outside and dislodge the insects with a spray of water; you could also dunk the whole plant in a bowl of tepid water. A sticky trap hung near the plant will trap large numbers of insects.*

Begonia leaf

FUNGUS GNATS

Also known as sciarid flies, these tiny brown or black insects fly around the plant. They aren't harmful but they are annoying. Their maggots mostly feed on organic matter in the compost but can sometimes attack plants' roots. Healthy plants can withstand this, but young or weak ones won't.

❤️ TREAT IT *Allow the top 1–2cm (½–¾in) of compost to dry out before watering – this suits most plants anyway. A yellow sticky trap will attract the insects away from your plant. Cover the surface of the compost with a mulch of fine gravel or pebbles to prevent the gnats laying their eggs.*

LEAF MINERS

Look for brown, white, or opaque meandering trails on the leaves, where the grubs have "mined" them. There may also be white dots on the leaves.

❤️ TREAT IT *Remove the affected leaves. Spray with an insecticide.*

The grub tunnels through the layers of the leaf

Pot mum leaf (pp.54–55)

THRIPS

Also known as thunder flies, these tiny brown or black sap-sucking insects may be seen on plants that have spent time outdoors. Signs of infestation include dull, mottled leaves, silvery-white streaks on the leaves or flowers, and distorted growth.

❤️ TREAT IT *Sticky traps – especially blue ones – can reduce their numbers and can help you monitor the problem. Spray your plant with insecticide or try a biological control.*

Mottled patches

Croton leaf (p.119)

continued

RED SPIDER MITES

Look for bleached or speckled foliage, webbing between the leaves and stems, and leaf fall. If you look under the leaves with the aid of a magnifying glass, you'll see the mites.

TREAT IT *Spray with an insecticide or use a biological control. Red spider mites thrive in hot, dry conditions so mist your plants daily to raise humidity if the atmosphere is hot and dry. Be vigilant – use a magnifying glass to look for the mites on the underside of leaves.*

Ivy leaf (pp.80–81)

"Inspect your plant regularly and deal with problems before they escalate."

VINE WEEVILS

If your plant has collapsed and you haven't over- or underwatered it, vine weevil grubs could be the culprit. They're found in the compost of plants that have spent time outside. They munch on the plant's roots, bulb, or tuber, causing it to suddenly wilt.

TREAT IT *If your plant has been outside in summer, drench the compost with an insecticide or biological control in late summer or early autumn to kill any grubs. If they have eaten most of the roots, your plant will not recover.*

Look for grubs in the compost of your plant

Hen & chicks (pp.72–73)

APHIDS

Also known as greenflies, these can be green, black, grey, or orange. They gather on the tip of the stems and on flower buds, where they suck sap and secrete honeydew, which is then colonized by sooty mould. Aphids can also spread viruses.

TREAT IT *Rub them off by hand, dislodge with a spray of water, or spray with insecticide. Hanging a yellow sticky trap nearby can help.*

Nerve plant leaf (pp.78–79)

SCALE INSECTS

These limpet-like insects look like brown lumps on the stems and the undersides of leaves. They also excrete a sticky sap, which can lead to sooty mould. If not controlled, your plant will be weakened and the leaves will turn yellow.

TREAT IT *Rub them off, or spray the affected areas with insecticide (don't spray the leaves of ferns, as they are very sensitive to chemicals). You could also try a biological control.*

Scale insects cluster along the centre of the leaves

Umbrella tree leaf (pp.118–119)

MEALYBUGS

These white, slow-moving insects coated in white fluff are found in clusters on stems, in leaf joints, and under leaves. They suck sap and excrete sticky honeydew, which then gets colonized by sooty mould. An infestation can lead to yellowing leaves, leaf fall, and wilting.

TREAT IT *Wipe off the insects with a damp cloth or cotton bud soaked with insecticide. Alternatively, spray the whole plant with insecticide once a week. You could try a biological control. Mealybugs are hard to eradicate and it is often simpler to throw away severely infested plants.*

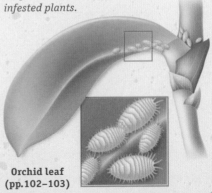

Orchid leaf (pp.102–103)

PLANT DISEASES

Caring for your houseplants correctly is the best defence against disease, but stay vigilant! Here's how to spot and treat diseases that could attack your plant.

Grey mould spreading

African violet (pp.112–113)

BOTRYTIS (OR GREY MOULD)

Grey fluff can be found all over the plant, especially in cool, damp, or congested conditions.

❤ **TREAT IT** *Water your plant from below to avoid splashing water on the leaves or crown. Remove any affected areas, along with any mouldy compost, and treat with a fungicide. Water and mist less frequently. Improve ventilation.*

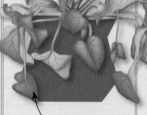

The plant has collapsed

Cyclamen (pp.60–61)

CROWN AND STEM ROT

The lower parts of the plant are dark, soft, and rotten, due to a fungal infection. It's usually caused by excess watering, splashing the base of the stems, or cool conditions.

❤ **TREAT IT** *You can try to save your plant by cutting out the affected area and treating it with a fungicide. Avoid overwatering, and move the plant to a warmer, well-ventilated spot.*

Patches of white dust

Missionary plant leaf (pp.108–109)

POWDERY MILDEW

Patches of white dust will appear on the leaves. It's more likely to occur where plants are crowded together, on underwatered plants, or in conditions that are too hot and humid. It's not fatal, but it can weaken your plant.

❤ **TREAT IT** *Remove the affected leaves, and treat your plant with fungicide. Space plants further apart to improve airflow.*

Corky growths

Radiator plant leaf
(pp.100–101)

OEDEMA

Look for corky growths on the underside of leaves. Oedema is caused by waterlogging, high humidity, and low light.

❤ **TREAT IT** *Water your plant less, reduce the humidity in the room, and move it to a brighter spot.*

Sooty mould

Umbrella tree leaf
(pp.118–119)

SOOTY MOULD

This black fungus grows on the sticky waste of aphids, whitefly, scale insects, and mealybugs. It blocks light and the plant's pores.

❤ **TREAT IT** *Sponge off the mould with a clean, damp cloth and treat the insect infestation (see Plant pests, pp.24–27).*

Mottled yellow markings

Indian rope plant leaf
(pp.88–89)

VIRUSES

Signs include mottled, yellow foliage, distorted growth, and white streaks on the flowers.

❤ **TREAT IT** *A virus would have been transmitted by insects or was already present on the plant when it was bought. There is nothing you can do to save it.*

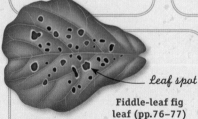

Leaf spot

Fiddle-leaf fig leaf (pp.76–77)

LEAF SPOT

Brown or black spots on the foliage are often surrounded by a yellow halo. Leaf spots can merge and kill an entire leaf. Caused by bacteria or fungi, they are more likely in damp or overcrowded conditions, or if water has been splashed on the leaves.

❤ **TREAT IT** *Remove any affected leaves and treat your plant with fungicide. Reduce humidity and space plants more widely.*

ROOT ROT

Caused by overwatering, root rot is a fungal infection of the roots that will lead to yellow, wilting leaves that turn brown, followed by the collapse of your plant. Affected roots will be soft and dark.

❤ **TREAT IT** *Remove the compost to check the roots. You can try to save it by trimming off any affected roots with a sharp knife, leaving any healthy, white roots. Then cut the plant back to allow for the root reduction, treat with a fungicide, and repot in fresh compost and a disinfected pot.*

Soft, rotten areas

Cactus (pp.98–99)

THE
HOUSEPLANTS

How to treasure
your houseplant
and deal with
any problems

MAIDENHAIR FERN

Adiantum raddianum

This delicate, arching fern is rather fussy and can be tricky to grow – it needs moisture, warmth, and a shady spot.

ı ı

HOW NOT TO KILL IT

LOCATION
Keep it at 15–21°C (60–70°F), and no colder than 10°C (50°F) in winter. Place it away from radiators and draughts. It needs a lot of humidity, so is good for a bathroom.

LIGHT
Keep it out of direct sunlight – about 1m (3ft) from a north window, or in the diffused light of an east-facing one.

WATERING + FEEDING
Water when the top 1cm (½in) of compost is dry, but let excess drain away – the compost should be moist. Feed once a month in spring or summer.

CARE
Place it on a pebble-filled tray of water and mist the leaves regularly to provide humidity – more often in a hot, dry room. Snip the old fronds off at the base.

> **BUG ALERT!**
> (see pp.24–27)
> Prone to **scale insects** and **mealybugs** on the foliage.

FRONDS TURNING BROWN AND CRISPY?

This is due to low humidity, draughts, close proximity to a radiator, bright sunlight, or because the compost is too dry.

SAVE IT *Snip off the affected fronds. Check your plant isn't in too bright a spot, or near a radiator. Mist your plant regularly and stand it on a tray of damp pebbles. Keep the compost moist.*

LEAVES TURNING PALE?

If the leaves are pale your plant may be in too much direct sun – in this case it may have scorch marks on the leaves too. Alternatively, it could also be in too dark a spot. Your plant may also need feeding.

☀ **SAVE IT** *Move it to a spot with diffused light. Feed your plant if you haven't been doing so.*

CRETAN BRAKE FERN
Pteris cretica

This fern needs similar care to a maidenhair fern, but is more forgiving if the compost dries out occasionally.

Adiantum raddianum
Height & spread: up to 40cm (16in)

YELLOW LEAVES?

This could be due to under- or overwatering, or exposure to temperature fluctuations.

♥ **SAVE IT** *Check that the compost isn't waterlogged and make sure your plant isn't near a radiator or air-conditioning unit.*

HARE'S FOOT FERN
Davillia canariensis

This fern has similar care needs but can cope with less water and less humidity.

URN PLANT

Aechmea fasciata

Urn plants are exotic-looking bromeliads that have long-lasting flowers. The rosette of leaves forms a central "vase" that holds water.

HOW **NOT** TO KILL IT

✓ LOCATION
Place the plant in a warm room that is 13–27°C (55–81°F). Good air circulation is important, so open a window on occasion.

LIGHT
Provide bright light, away from direct sun, which will burn the leaves.

WATERING + FEEDING
Water the central vase, ensuring the water is always 2–3cm (1in) deep. Use distilled, filtered, or rainwater. Empty and refill the vase every 2–3 weeks to prevent the water stagnating. Water the compost in summer if the top 2–3cm (1in) is dry. Allow to drain after.

CARE
Provide high humidity if the room is warm – place it on a pebble-filled tray of water and mist the leaves 1–2 times a week.

BUG ALERT! (see pp.24–27)	Prone to **mealybugs** and **scale insects** on the foliage.

BROWN, SOGGY LEAVES OR WILTING LEAVES?

This could be crown or root rot, caused by overwatering or poor drainage.

SAVE IT *Check for crown and root rot. Try trimming off the affected areas, treating with fungicide, and repotting in fresh compost. For more information, see Plant diseases (pp.28–29).*

— Brown leaf

FLOWER OR PLANT DYING BACK?

This is normal.

SAVE IT *Cut away the flower, as near to the foliage as you can, using a sharp knife. Urn plants only flower once, but if you continue to care for your plant it will produce "pups" (new plants at its base). When they are a third the size of the main plant, cut them away carefully and pot them up individually.*

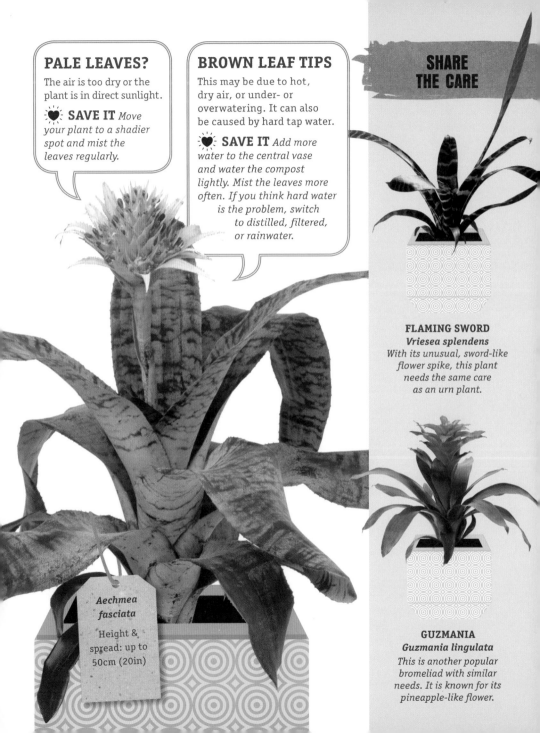

PALE LEAVES?

The air is too dry or the plant is in direct sunlight.

💖 **SAVE IT** *Move your plant to a shadier spot and mist the leaves regularly.*

BROWN LEAF TIPS

This may be due to hot, dry air, or under- or overwatering. It can also be caused by hard tap water.

💖 **SAVE IT** *Add more water to the central vase and water the compost lightly. Mist the leaves more often. If you think hard water is the problem, switch to distilled, filtered, or rainwater.*

SHARE THE CARE

FLAMING SWORD
Vriesea splendens
With its unusual, sword-like flower spike, this plant needs the same care as an urn plant.

GUZMANIA
Guzmania lingulata
This is another popular bromeliad with similar needs. It is known for its pineapple-like flower.

Aechmea fasciata

Height & spread: up to 50cm (20in)

ELEPHANT'S EAR

Alocasia x amazonica

Elephant's ears like hot, steamy conditions and have impressive, veined, dark green leaves.

||||||||||||||||||||||||||||||||||||||||||||||||||

HOW **NOT** TO KILL IT

✓ LOCATION
Keep the plant at a temperature of 18–21°C (65–70°F) all year round. Avoid placing it near radiators, air conditioning units, and cold draughts.

LIGHT
Keep the plant out of direct sun in summer – a partially shaded spot is best. In winter, move it to a brighter spot.

WATERING + FEEDING
Keep the compost moist (but not soggy) by watering lightly every few days. Use distilled, filtered, or rainwater that is tepid. Feed once a month during spring and summer. Water more sparingly in winter.

CARE
Alocasias love high humidity, so stand the plant on a pebble-filled tray of water and mist the leaves frequently. Ensure that the pot has good drainage. Repot in spring, but only if the roots are significantly outgrowing the pot.

BROWN PATCHES ON THE LEAVES?

This is sunburn.

☀ **SAVE IT** *Move your plant to a more shaded spot, out of direct sunlight.*

Brown patches

PLANT DYING BACK?

If it is winter, your plant is probably going dormant, especially if temperatures fall below 15°C (60°F). If it isn't winter, it's not happy with its conditions.

☀ **SAVE IT** *If dormant, your plant should re-sprout in spring – continue to care for it as normal. Otherwise, check location, light, and watering regimes (see left).*

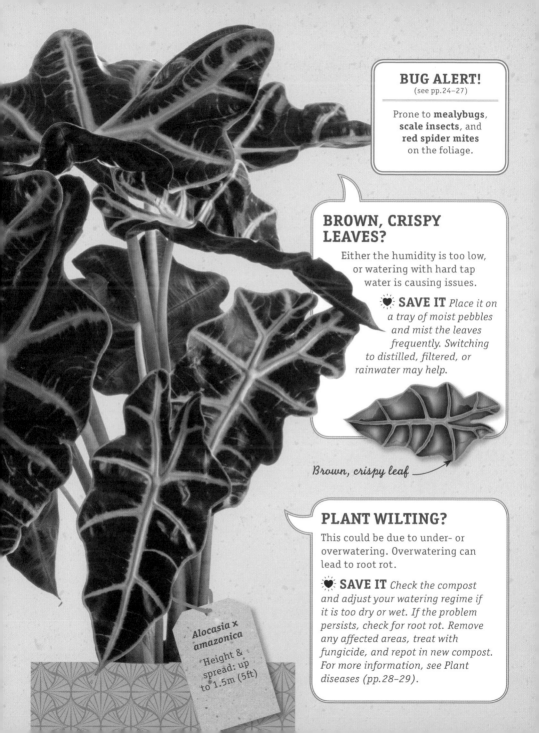

BUG ALERT!
(see pp.24–27)

Prone to **mealybugs**, **scale insects**, and **red spider mites** on the foliage.

BROWN, CRISPY LEAVES?

Either the humidity is too low, or watering with hard tap water is causing issues.

🖤 **SAVE IT** *Place it on a tray of moist pebbles and mist the leaves frequently. Switching to distilled, filtered, or rainwater may help.*

Brown, crispy leaf

PLANT WILTING?

This could be due to under- or overwatering. Overwatering can lead to root rot.

🖤 **SAVE IT** *Check the compost and adjust your watering regime if it is too dry or wet. If the problem persists, check for root rot. Remove any affected areas, treat with fungicide, and repot in new compost. For more information, see Plant diseases (pp.28–29).*

Alocasia x amazonica

Height & spread: up to 1.5m (5ft)

ALOE VERA

Aloe vera

This easy-to-grow succulent has spiky, fleshy leaves. The sap is used to soothe burns and skin irritations.

BUG ALERT!
(see pp.24–27)

Prone to **scale insects** on the foliage.

HOW **NOT** TO KILL IT

LOCATION
Keep it in a room that is 10–24°C (50–75°F). Happy, mature plants will produce yellow flowers.

LIGHT
Place in a bright spot (e.g. a south-facing window). It will cope with some direct sun, but acclimatize it gradually.

WATERING + FEEDING
In spring and summer, water when the top 2–3cm (1in) of compost has dried out – this may be once a week, depending on its position. In winter, water very sparingly. Feed once in spring and once in summer.

CARE
Aloes like well-drained compost, so add potting grit or perlite when planting, or use cactus compost. A layer of grit on the top will keep the neck dry and prevent rot. Only repot if the plant has outgrown its pot. The plant will produce baby "offsets" – these can be left on the plant, or cut off at the base with their roots and planted individually.

SHRUNKEN, WRINKLED LEAVES?
Your plant needs watering.

☀ **SAVE IT** *Water lightly and mist the leaves. Do the same the following day, and the day after that – the leaves should plump up again. Don't let your plant sit in very wet compost.*

LEAVES TURNING BROWN, RED, OR REDDISH BROWN?
Your plant could be getting too much sun in the middle of the day during summer, or it may be overwatered. The roots may also be damaged.

☀ **SAVE IT** *Move your plant to a bright spot with less direct sunlight. Reduce watering. If it doesn't recover, check the roots.*

— *Reddish brown leaf*

PALE OR YELLOWING LEAVES?

If your whole plant is pale or yellowing, it has been overwatered, or it isn't getting enough light.

☀ **SAVE IT** *Ensure that you are watering the plant correctly (see left). Move it to a brighter spot.*

DARK SPOTS? BROWN OR MUSHY LEAVES?

This is most likely due to overwatering.

☀ **SAVE IT** *Do not water until the compost has dried out. Ensure that the pot has drainage holes. Avoid spilling water on the foliage, as it will gather at the base and cause rot.*

Dark spots ←

Aloe vera
Height & spread: up to 1m (3ft)

AGAVE
Agave
Ideal for a sunny windowsill, this succulent needs the same care as an aloe. Some varieties have very sharp spines.

HAWORTHIA
Haworthia
Another spiky succulent with the same care needs. In direct sun, the leaves may turn red.

FLAMINGO FLOWER

Anthurium

Also called oilcloth flower, this easy-to-grow houseplant has wavy, exotic, brightly coloured flowers (spathes) that can last for weeks.

HOW NOT TO KILL IT

LOCATION
A flamingo flower is a tropical plant, so needs warmth and humidity. Place the plant in a warm room (15–20°C/60–68°F) and away from draughts.

LIGHT
Position it in bright light, but out of direct sun, such as 1m (3ft) or so away from a sunny window.

WATERING + FEEDING
Water moderately from spring to autumn, whenever the soil surface feels dry. After watering, the compost should feel moist but not soggy. Water less in winter. Feed monthly in spring and summer.

CARE
To provide humidity, mist the leaves regularly (avoiding the flowers) or stand the plant on a pebble-filled tray of water. Clean the leaves frequently with a damp sponge, and gently pull off spent flowers. Repot in spring into a slightly larger pot.

BUG ALERT!
(see pp.24–27)

Prone to **mealybugs** and **red spider mites** on the foliage.

Sunburn marks

LEAF TIPS GOING BROWN?

The air isn't humid enough or your plant has too much direct sunlight – the leaves can burn easily.

SAVE IT *Increase humidity by misting the leaves regularly, or place the pot on a pebble-filled tray of water. Move to a bright spot that is out of direct sunlight.*

Anthurium andraeanum

Height & spread: up to 50cm (20in)

LOTS OF LEAVES BUT NO FLOWERS?

Your plant may not be getting enough sunlight, it might be in too large a pot, or it may be underfed.

SAVE IT *Move to a brighter spot. Repot in a smaller pot if there is more than 1–2cm (½–¾in) between the edge of the pot and the root ball. Feed once a month to encourage flowering (see left).*

YELLOWING LEAVES?

This could be due to too much watering or overfeeding.

SAVE IT *Don't allow your plant to sit in water, and only water again when the top of the compost is dry. If necessary, stop feeding for a month or two.*

EMERALD FERN

Asparagus densiflorus Sprengeri Group

Not actually a fern but a member of the lily family, this easy-care plant has graceful, feathery foliage.

| | | | | | | | | | | | | | | | | | | | | | | | | | | | | | | | | | | | | | | | | | | | | | | | | | | | | | | | | | | | | |

HOW **NOT** TO KILL IT

LOCATION
Place the plant in a coolish room (7–21°C/45–70°F), away from direct heat, such as a radiator. It likes some humidity, so does well grouped with other plants. It's a good choice for a bathroom.

LIGHT
Ideally, provide bright, indirect light.

WATERING + FEEDING
Water when the top 2–3cm (1in) of compost has dried out. Don't let the compost dry out completely, or allow it to become waterlogged. Reduce watering in winter. Feed monthly in spring and summer.

CARE
In winter, mist the leaves occasionally if the room is centrally heated. Cut away any yellowing stems at the base. Repot the plant in spring if the root ball comes into contact with the edge of the pot.

Asparagus densiflorus Sprengeri Group
Height & spread: up to 30cm (12in)

YELLOW FOLIAGE?

Older foliage at the bottom of the plant will yellow naturally. If yellowing is widespread, the room temperature may be too high, there may be too much light, or your plant may be under- or overwatered. Ensure the compost is not waterlogged, as this leads to root rot.

☀ **SAVE IT** *Move it away from a radiator or to a cooler room, and place it in a slightly shadier spot. Allow the compost to dry out if it is waterlogged and ensure you let the top 2–3cm (1in) dry out between waterings. Check for root rot (see Plant diseases, pp.28–29).*

Widespread yellowing

BUG ALERT!
(see pp.24–27)

Prone to **red spider mites** on the foliage.

BROWN EDGES ON THE LEAVES?

Your plant has had too much sun, or the compost has dried out.

♥ **SAVE IT** *Move it to a shadier spot. Water, letting any excess drain away.*

Brown leaves

ASPARAGUS FERN
Asparagus setaceus
It has similar care needs, but this plant likes higher humidity than its cousin and can tolerate less light.

SHAMROCK PLANT
Oxalis triangularis
This pretty plant has similar care requirements. It is a bulb, so dies back in winter.

PAINTED-LEAF BEGONIA

Begonia rex

There are many varieties of painted-leaf begonia that have beautiful foliage in shades of crimson, silver, purple, green, and red.

HOW NOT TO KILL IT

LOCATION
Ideally, keep the plant at around 18–21°C (64–70°F) all year round, but don't let it get any hotter. They can survive at 13°C (55°F) in winter, but no colder.

LIGHT
Place it in good, but indirect light. Avoid direct sun, which can burn the leaves.

WATERING + FEEDING
Water so the compost is moist, but allow it to dry out a little in between waterings during summer. It is best watered from below to stop water accumulating at the base of the stems (see Water it, pp.20–21). Keep just moist in winter.

CARE
Repot if necessary in spring. Turn the pot regularly to ensure the plant grows evenly. Make sure it has good ventilation.

BUG ALERT! (see pp.24–27) Prone to **aphids**, **red spider mites**, **whitefly** and **thrips**.

WHITE POWDER ON THE LEAVES?

This is powdery mildew, often due to drought or too much heat, humid conditions, or poor air circulation.

♥ **SAVE IT** *Remove the affected leaves and treat with fungicide. For more information, see Plant diseases (pp.28–29).*

White powder

LOSING LEAVES?

Your plant may be overwatered, or too hot. If it's going leggy too, it doesn't have enough light.

♥ **SAVE IT** *Move it to a brighter spot, out of direct sunlight. Check the temperature and your watering regime (see left).*

YELLOWING LEAVES?

These could be due to too much or too little water, or not enough light.

❤ **SAVE IT** *Check your plant's care regime and position (see left).*

GREY FLUFF ON PARTS OF THE PLANT?

This is grey mould (botrytis), due to cool, damp, crowded conditions, or water splashing onto the leaves.

❤ **SAVE IT** *Move the plant away from other begonias to stop the infection spreading and improve ventilation. Remove any affected areas and treat with fungicide (see Plant diseases, pp.28-29).*

SHARE THE CARE

ELIATOR HYBRIDS
Begonia Eliator Group
These have small, pretty flowers in a range of colours. Deadhead regularly to prolong flowering.

TUBEROUS BEGONIAS
Begonia spp.
Deadhead regularly to prolong flowering. At the end of the season, cut back your plant, remove the compost from the tuber, store in a cool, dry place over winter, and repot in spring.

Begonia rex
Height: up to 60cm (24in)
Spread: up to 45cm (18in)

TOP 5 PLANTS FOR
YOUR DESK

Greening up your workspace is said to boost productivity and reduce stress, with scientific studies revealing that certain plants can remove toxins from the air. A good desk plant is compact, and not too fussy about light levels.

Lucky bamboo
Dracaena sanderiana

We can't guarantee that this plant will get you a pay rise or a promotion, but it will bring cheer to your working day. Grow it in compost or even just in a glass of distilled, filtered, or rainwater.

See Lucky bamboo, pp.70–71.

Blushing bromeliad
Neoregelia carolinae f. tricolor

This attractive plant is grown for its foliage, which blushes pink just before it flowers. Keep its central "vase" topped up with bottled water.

See Blushing bromeliad, p.49.

African spear

Sansevieria cylindrica

This striking foliage plant is related to the spiky snake plant, and has cylindrical leaves. It's a low maintenance plant that doesn't need much watering – so it can tolerate a bit of neglect if you go away.

See African spear, p.115.

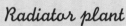

Radiator plant

Peperomia metallica

Peperomias are attractive foliage plants. They are a great choice for your desk at work as they are compact, and do well under the fluorescent lights of office buildings.

See Radiator plant, pp.100–101.

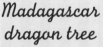

Madagascar dragon tree

Dracaena marginata

This easy-going plant is a good air purifier, and doesn't mind erratic watering. It can get quite tall, but it doesn't take up much room as it has a very thin trunk. Keep it in a lightly shaded spot.

See Dragon tree, p.69.

QUEEN'S TEARS

Billbergia nutans

This is one of the easiest bromeliads to grow. Try displaying queen's tears in a hanging planter.

HOW **NOT** TO KILL IT

LOCATION
Keep the plant in a room that is 5–24°C (41–75°F). It will only flower if at the upper end of this range.

LIGHT
Place in bright, but indirect light.

WATERING + FEEDING
Water the "vase" (the centre of the rosette of leaves) with distilled, filtered, or rainwater, ensuring the water is always 2–3cm (1in) deep. Empty and refill the vase every 2–3 weeks to prevent the water stagnating. Keep the compost just moist. Feed once a month in spring and summer by adding half-strength liquid feed to the central vase.

CARE

Place the plant on a pebble-filled tray of water for humidity. It will flower at around 3 years old. Gently pull faded flowers away. Repot after flowering in spring. It will produce "pups" (new plants at the base), dying slowly in the process. Pot up pups when they are one-third the size of the parent.

LEAF TIPS TURNING YELLOW?
Your plant has probably outgrown its container.

❤ **SAVE IT** *Repot your plant in spring, after it has flowered.*

BROWN LEAF TIPS?

This could be due to dry air, or watering with hard water.

❤ **SAVE IT** *Mist the leaves regularly, if warm. Switch to distilled, filtered, or rainwater.*

DRIPPING FLOWERS?

This is nectar, which drips from the flowers when they are moved or touched – hence *Billbergia*'s common name, queen's tears.

❤ **SAVE IT** *Do nothing!*

SHARE THE CARE

PINK QUILL
Tillandsia cyanea
This bromeliad has similar care needs to queen's tears, but prefers a warmer room (14–25°C/57–77°F).

BLUSHING BROMELIAD
Neoregelia carolinae
f. *tricolor*
Provide the same care as for pink quill. The central vase turns red ("blushes") before it flowers.

Billbergia nutans
Height & spread: up to 50cm (20in)

NO FLOWERS?

Your plant won't flower until it's around 3 years old. If you have a mature plant, the temperature may be too low, or it may be in too dark a spot.

❤ **SAVE IT** *Move it to a warmer spot in a bright position. Avoid placing it in direct sunlight.*

PEACOCK PLANT

Calathea

Most peacock plants are grown for their leaves. Calathea roseopicta leaves have red undersides.

||||||||||||||||||||||||||||||

HOW **NOT** TO KILL IT

✓ LOCATION
It is a rainforest plant, so keep it in a warm room (16–20°C/60–68°F). It needs humidity, so a bathroom can be ideal. Avoid rooms with sudden temperature fluctuations.

LIGHT
Put it in partial shade or bright light. Keep it away from direct sun.

WATERING + FEEDING
From spring to autumn, keep the compost moist (but not wet) at all times. Use distilled, filtered, or rainwater as these plants are sensitive to chemicals added to tap water. Ensure the pot drains well. Water more sparingly in winter. Feed once in spring, summer, and autumn.

CARE
To maintain humidity, stand it on a pebble-filled tray of water, and mist daily. Grouping with other plants will also improve humidity. Wipe the leaves occasionally to keep them free of dust. Repot in spring.

Calathea roseopicta
Height: up to 24cm (9½in)
Spread: up to 15cm (6in)

DROOPY LEAVES?

This could be a sign of overwatering. Alternatively, your plant may be too cold or exposed to draughts.

SAVE IT *The compost should be moist but not wet. Water sparingly in winter. Try moving your plant to a warmer, sheltered spot.*

BUG ALERT!
(see pp.24–27)

Prone to **red spider mites** on the foliage.

Brown leaf edge

LEAF TIPS OR EDGES BROWN?

The air is probably too dry, you may have overfed your plant, or it may be due to watering with hard water.

SAVE IT *Mist your plant daily and place it on a pebble-filled tray of water. Group with other plants to increase humidity. Switch to distilled, filtered, or rainwater.*

FADED OR SCORCHED LEAVES?

Your plant has probably been in direct sunlight.

SAVE IT *Move it to a shadier place.*

Faded leaf

SPIDER PLANT

Chlorophytum comosum

Spider plants are ideal for beginners as they are very easy to care for. Display them in a hanging planter.

HOW **NOT** TO KILL IT

LOCATION
Keep the plant in a room that is always between 7–24°C (45–75°F).

LIGHT
Place it in a bright spot, away from direct sunlight.

WATERING + FEEDING
Keep the compost moist but not soggy. Water more sparingly in winter. Feed every few weeks except during winter.

CARE
Repot young plants into a slightly bigger pot every spring. Repot mature plants when the white, fleshy roots begin to push the plant from its container, making it tricky to water. Mature spider plants produce "plantlets" or "babies" that can be cut off and grown individually. If they have tiny roots, plant them directly into new compost. If they have no roots, place them in water for a few weeks until the roots appear.

BROWN TIPS ON THE LEAVES?

Your plant can tolerate the hot, dry air of centrally heated rooms, but this may make the leaf tips go brown. Underfeeding or underwatering can have the same effect.

SAVE IT *Cut off the brown tips and move your plant to a cooler room. Make sure you feed and water it regularly.*

BROWN STREAKS ON THE LEAVES IN WINTER?

This means your plant has been watered too much in cool conditions.

SAVE IT *Remove any unsightly leaves. Make sure that you water your plant less during winter – the compost should be just moist.*

brown streaks

YELLOW LEAVES?

The soil around the roots is too dry, which might mean your plant needs repotting. Alternatively, it may have root rot.

☀️❤️ **SAVE IT** *Remove any unsightly leaves. Water well from spring to autumn. Repot your plant if it is bulging from its pot. Check for root rot (see Plant diseases, pp.28–29).*

PALE LEAVES?

Harsh sunlight, lack of water, or low sunlight and low temperatures in winter can all make the leaves turn pale.

☀️❤️ **SAVE IT** *Move the plant out of direct sunlight, and water well. In winter, move your plant to a warmer, brighter room.*

SHARE THE CARE

POTHOS
Epipremnum
This plant has similar needs to a spider plant, and will climb up a moss pole or trail from a pot.

ARROWHEAD PLANT
Syngonium podophyllum
Care for as you would a spider plant. It will climb or trail, and looks great in a hanging planter.

Chlorophytum comosum
Height: up to 20cm (8in)
Spread: up to 30cm (12in)

POT MUM

Chrysanthemum

Blooms come in many colours and last for several weeks. Choose plants with both open flowers and opening buds.

BUG ALERT!
(see pp.24–27)

Prone to **aphids**, **leaf miners**, and **red spider mites** on the foliage.

HOW NOT TO KILL IT

LOCATION
Keep the plant at 10–15°C (50–60°F), as the flowers will last longer. A windowsill in a cool room is ideal.

LIGHT
Provide bright, indirect light; keep it out of direct sun.

WATERING + FEEDING
A pot mum likes water, so keep the compost moist (but not soggy) at all times. You could feed the plant after a few weeks. It won't flower for long enough to need feeding a second time.

CARE
Deadhead any spent flowers. Plants are often discarded after flowering, but you could try planting yours in the garden. It will have been treated with dwarfing hormones before it was sold, but should revert to its normal growth habit outdoors, and may flower in autumn.

WILTING LEAVES?
The plant needs watering.

SAVE IT *Water your plant and ensure you are keeping the compost moist, but not soggy.*

Wilting leaves

FLOWERS NOT LASTING?

Higher temperatures will make the flowers open more rapidly and fade more quickly.

❤ **SAVE IT** *Move it to a cooler spot that is 10–15°C (50–60°F).*

FUZZY GREY MOULD ON THE FOLIAGE?

This grey mould is called botrytis, and may have been caused by your plant sitting in its cellophane wrapping for a long time.

❤ **SAVE IT** *Remove any affected areas and treat with fungicide. For more information, see Plant diseases (pp.28–29).*

Fuzzy grey mould

Chrysanthemum
Height & spread: up to 30cm (12in)

BUDS WON'T OPEN?

The plant may not be getting enough light. If the buds are completely green, they may not open.

❤ **SAVE IT** *Move your plant to a brighter spot.*

MINIATURE ROSES
Rosa

Potted roses should last for weeks indoors if cared for like pot mums. Try planting them in the garden after flowering. They go dormant in winter.

PRIMROSE
Primula vulgaris

These bring some welcome colour to the home in winter and spring. Care for them in the same way, and once they have finished flowering, plant them in the garden.

NATAL LILY

Clivia miniata

Natal lilies are native to South Africa and produce a beautiful, single, red, orange, or yellow flower in early spring.

HOW **NOT** TO KILL IT

LOCATION
From spring to late autumn, keep the plant in a heated room. In winter, move it to a room that is 10°C (50°F) for 3 months to rest – this will help initiate a flower bud. Then return it to its spring-to-autumn position.

LIGHT
Provide bright, but indirect light.

WATERING + FEEDING
From spring to late autumn, keep the compost moist. Reduce watering in winter so that the compost is almost dry. Feed once a month from spring to autumn, and not at all during winter.

CARE
Wipe the leaves occasionally. Don't move the pot when the plant is flowering or in bud. After flowering, cut off the dead flower spike at the base. The plant may produce a second flower in late summer. Natal lilies like to be snug, so repot the plant after flowering only if the roots are bursting out of the pot.

BLEACHED OR BROWN PATCHES ON THE LEAVES?

The leaves are sunburnt.

💗 **SAVE IT** *Move your plant out of direct sunlight.*

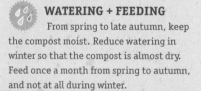
Bleached patches on the leaves

BUG ALERT!
(see pp.24–27) | Prone to **mealybugs** and **red spider mites** on the foliage.

BROWN LEAVES AT THE BASE OF YOUR PLANT?

This happens when the older leaves are dying back.

💗 **SAVE IT** *This is normal, just gently pull away any brown leaves.*

YELLOW LEAVES?

This could be due to underfeeding, or under- or overwatering.

☀💜 **SAVE IT** *Ensure you are using the correct watering and feeding regime for the season (see left).*

Yellow leaves

SHORT FLOWER SPIKE?
NO FLOWER IN SPRING?

This is most likely due to a lack of rest in winter, but it could be because the pot is too large, or because your plant was underwatered after being rested.

💜 **SAVE IT** *If it has been rested, ensure you keep the compost moist. Check the pot is not too big – the root ball should only be 2–3cm (1in) away from the edge of the pot.*

Clivia miniata

Height: up to 45cm (18in)

Spread: up to 30cm (12in)

MONEY PLANT

Crassula ovata

This low-maintenance, long-lasting succulent looks like a tiny tree and is said to bring good fortune. It can produce flowers in winter.

HOW **NOT** TO KILL IT

 LOCATION
Position the plant on a sunny windowsill that is 18–24°C (50–75°F). It will tolerate periods at 10°C (50°F) in winter.

LIGHT
Provide bright, dappled sunlight.

 WATERING + FEEDING
Water moderately; let the top 2–3cm (1in) of compost dry out between waterings. Water more sparingly in winter. Feed once in spring and then again in summer.

CARE
Pull off any old, shrivelled leaves. In spring, lightly prune the plant to shape. Plant it in a weighty pot as it can become top-heavy and topple over.

BUG ALERT!
(see pp.24–27)

Prone to **mealybugs** on the stems and leaves.

YELLOWING LEAVES?

This is probably due to overwatering.

☀ **SAVE IT** *Allow the compost to dry out and check that the pot is well drained.*

DROPPING LEAVES?

Older leaves will shrivel and fall off naturally, but younger leaves may drop under environmental stress (such as being moved to bright sunlight suddenly, or over- or underwatering).

♥ **SAVE IT** *Give water if the compost is very dry, or allow it to dry out if soggy. When repositioning, move your plant gradually towards the desired spot over a week, to allow it to acclimatize.*

 Dropped leaves

SHRIVELLED LEAVES AND STEMS?

Your plant is short of water.

☀❤ SAVE IT *Give your plant a small amount of water daily over the course of a few days – the leaves should soon plump up again. Don't let it stand in sodden compost.*

Shrivelled leaves ➜

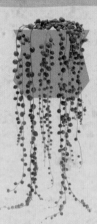

STRING OF BEADS
Senecio rowleyanus
This eye-catching, hanging plant has similar needs to a money plant.

Crassula ovata

Height & spread: up to 1m (3ft)

LEGGY PLANT?

Your plant needs more sunlight.

☀❤ SAVE IT *Move it to a sunnier spot.*

HEARTS ON A STRING
Ceropegia woodii
This fleshy-leaved plant has similar needs and is great for a hanging planter.

FLORISTS' CYCLAMEN

Cyclamen persicum

Cyclamen makes a charming indoor plant, adorned from autumn to spring with bright flowers.

HOW **NOT** TO KILL IT

LOCATION
A cyclamen should flower for several months in a cool room, if bought in bud in autumn (the start of the flowering season). It won't like high temperatures, but don't let it freeze either – keeping it at 10–15°C (50–60°F) is best.

LIGHT
Keep out of direct sunlight – a north-facing windowsill would be ideal.

WATERING + FEEDING
Keep the compost just moist, watering from below by standing the plant in a saucer of water for about 30 minutes (see Water it pp.18–19). This avoids getting the leaves and stems wet.

CARE
Remove spent flowers or dead leaves by giving them a sharp tug or snipping them off. Most plants are discarded after they flower, but it is possible to keep them going from year to year (see No more flowers?).

Yellowed leaf

YELLOW FOLIAGE?

Your plant is too warm, has been over- or underwatered, or exposed to direct sunlight. If it's spring, it may be dying back naturally.

SAVE IT *Remove yellow leaves. Move it out of direct sunlight, and to a place around 15°C (60°F). Keep the compost just moist, watering from below (see Water it, pp.18–19).*

POOR FLOWERING?

Your plant will flower best in lower temperatures, as high temperatures will send it into early dormancy. If it's nearing the end of the season, your plant will stop flowering.

❤ **SAVE IT** *Check your plant isn't in too warm a spot to flower, and ensure you are caring for it correctly (see left). Buy cyclamen in autumn and look for plants with lots of buds. These will be the longest-flowering plants as the buds will open into new flowers as the older ones fade.*

INDIAN AZALEA
Rhododendron simsii
Care for an Indian azalea in the same way as a cyclamen, keeping the compost moist and watering them with soft water or rainwater as they don't like lime. Needs a cool spot to flower well.

PLANT HAS COLLAPSED?

This is probably because your plant is getting too much water, and may be due to crown rot.

❤ **SAVE IT** *Look for crown rot at the base of the stems; remove affected areas. For more information, see Plant diseases (pp.28–29). Crown rot is likely to kill your plant.*

Crown rot

Cyclamen persicum
Height: up to 20cm (8in)
Spread: up to 15cm (6in)

NO MORE FLOWERS?

Florists' cyclamen dies back and goes dormant over summer.

❤ **SAVE IT** *Stop watering your plant when it stops flowering and the leaves turn yellow and wither in spring. Place your plant outside in a dry, shaded place over summer, keeping the compost just moist. If you live in a wet area, put the pot on its side so that any rainwater drains out. In autumn, bring the plant back indoors and, when you see regrowth, start watering again.*

DUMB CANE

Dieffenbachia

Dumb cane (or leopard lily) acquired its name from its poison, which temporarily causes speech loss. It is known for its lush foliage.

❚❚❚

HOW NOT TO KILL IT

LOCATION
Keep it in a warm room that is 16–24°C (60–75°F). Dumb canes are a little fussy, and don't like cold draughts or dry air.

LIGHT
Place it in a partially shaded spot in summer. Move it to a brighter spot in winter.

WATERING + FEEDING
From spring to autumn, water whenever the top 2–3cm (1in) of compost is dry. Water sparingly in winter. Feed once a month.

CARE
Provide humidity by misting the leaves regularly and placing the plant on a pebble-filled tray of water. Wipe the leaves once a month. Repot in spring.

BUG ALERT!
(see pp.24–27)
Prone to **mealybugs** on the foliage.

YELLOWING LOWER LEAVES?
Low temperatures or draughts are probably the reason.

☀ **SAVE IT** *Move it to a warmer room, somewhere free of draughts.*

PALE LEAVES?
Too much bright light or direct sun will make the leaves look bleached and washed out.

☀ **SAVE IT** *Move your plant to a shadier spot.*

LEAVES DROPPING?

The room may be too cold or draughty for your plant.

☀ **SAVE IT** *Check for draughts and place your plant in a warmer location.*

BROWN EDGES ON THE LEAVES?

The compost may be too dry, or either dry or cold air may be the cause. Another possibility is that your plant has been given too much fertilizer.

☀ **SAVE IT** *Water until the compost feels moist but not soggy, and allow only the top 2–3cm (1in) of compost to dry out between waterings. Increase the humidity around your plant, move it to a warmer spot, and check your feeding regime (see left).*

Dieffenbachia seguine

Height & spread: up to 60cm (24in)

HEART-LEAF PHILODENDRON
Philodendron scandens

Usually sold climbing a moss pole, this glossy-leaved plant can tolerate shady spots. Care for as you would a dumb cane.

BLUSHING PHILODENDRON
Philodendron erubescens

This slow-growing climber has similar needs. It has purple leaves when young.

VENUS FLY TRAP

Dionaea muscipula

This fascinating, carnivorous plant has traps that snap shut when an insect lands on them. The captured insect is then slowly digested.

HOW **NOT** TO KILL IT

LOCATION
Place the plant on a south-facing windowsill in a moderately warm room (7–21°C/45–70°F). In winter, rest it in an unheated room (7°C/45°F).

LIGHT
Provide bright sunlight, some direct.

WATERING + FEEDING
Keep the compost moist in the growing season (sit it in a saucer of water), and just moist during its resting period. Use distilled, filtered, or rainwater. Do not use fertilizer as the plant gets its nutrients from the insects it catches. If there are no insects indoors, place it outside for a few days at a time during summer to catch prey.

CARE
Plant it in a very low-nutrient, specialist-mix compost. Cut off the dead traps with scissors. The plant may flower in summer. It's best to cut off the flowers as these will weaken the plant. Repot if necessary in early spring.

Green, floppy lobes

RED LOBES TURNING GREEN AND FLOPPY?

This is a sign that your plant isn't happy with your watering regime or humidity. The plant may die suddenly if this is not remedied quickly.

SAVE IT *Increase humidity by misting the leaves. Check your watering regime (see left).*

BLACKENED TRAPS?

Traps often die off in autumn and winter as the plant goes dormant.

SAVE IT *This is normal. When the plant comes back into growth after the winter, it will produce new traps.*

YELLOW, BROWN, OR BLACK TRAPS?

This can happen if your plant is moved from a shady spot to a very sunny one too quickly.

☀ **SAVE IT** *Acclimatize your plant to brighter spots gradually over the course of a week.*

← *Burnt leaves*

TRAP NOT CLOSING?

This is likely to be the result of curious fingers poking at your plant too many times.

♥ **SAVE IT** *Each trap will only close four or five times in its lifetime, so resist "teasing" your plant.*

BUG ALERT!
(see pp. 24–27)

Prone to **aphids** and **red spider mites**.

Dionaea muscipula
Height: up to 45cm (18in)
Spread: up to 15cm (6in)

PITCHER PLANT
Sarracenia
This plant attracts insects that fall into it and drown. It has the same needs as a venus fly trap.

MONKEY CUPS
Nepenthes
Insects are trapped in the brightly coloured pitchers of this plant. Care for it as you would a venus fly trap.

TOP 5 PLANTS FOR
SUNNY SPOTS

The sun's rays can scorch the foliage of many houseplants, but some plants, including desert cacti and succulents, love sunshine. Acclimatize them gradually and shade them from very strong midday sun in summer. They look great grouped together – here are five to try.

Hen & chicks
Echeveria

This rosette-forming succulent can cope with some direct sunlight. A hen & chicks will produce pretty, yellow, orange, or pink, bell-shaped flowers.

See Hen & chicks, pp.72–73.

Desert cactus
Opuntia

Cacti come in a fascinating range of shapes and sizes. This cactus is native to the arid regions of North, Central, and South America – it is therefore no surprise it loves bright light!

See Desert cacti, pp.98–99.

Money plant
Crassula ovata

This plant needs lots of bright light, and can tolerate some direct sunlight. It is often quite small when bought, so is perfect for a sunny windowsill. It will last many years and may produce small flowers each winter.

See Money plant, pp.58–59.

Aloe vera
Aloe vera

This spiky succulent enjoys being in a very bright location, and can even cope with some direct sunlight. A mature aloe will produce offsets (new baby plants) at its base.

See Aloe vera, pp.38–39.

Venus fly trap
Dionaea muscipula

This fun plant needs lots of bright light and some direct sunlight. When an insect lands on the hinged leaves, they snap shut, trapping the prey inside.

See Venus fly trap, pp.64–65.

DRAGON TREE

Dracaena fragrans

Grown for their palm-like leaves, dragon trees are easy-going, indoor shrubs that don't mind erratic watering.

HOW **NOT** TO KILL IT

 LOCATION
Place the plant close to an east- or west-facing window in a room that is 13–21°C (55–70°F).

 LIGHT
Keep it out of direct sunlight.

WATERING + FEEDING
From spring to autumn, water freely when the top 2–3cm (1in) of the compost has become dry. In winter, keep the compost just moist. Feed monthly from spring to autumn, but not during winter. They can survive irregular watering to a certain extent.

CARE
Wipe the leaves occasionally, pulling away any that are dead. The plant needs humidity, so place it on a pebble-filled tray of water and mist a few times a week.

BUG ALERT!
(see pp.24–27)
Look for **mealybugs** and **scale insects** on the foliage.

WILTING LEAVES?

You may be watering your plant too little or too much. It may also have root rot.

SAVE IT *Make sure you are watering correctly (see left). Check the pot has good drainage. If the problem persists, check for root rot and remove any affected areas. For more information, see Plant diseases (pp.28–29).*

BROWN TIPS ON THE LEAVES?

This is probably due to dry air, but it could be due to your plant getting too little water.

☀ **SAVE IT** *Increase humidity and make sure that you water your plant correctly for the season (see left).*

YELLOWING LEAVES AT THE BASE?

Each leaf will naturally turn yellow and fall off after a couple of years.

☀ **SAVE IT** *Don't worry! Just gently pull away the yellowed leaves to remove them.*

Yellowing leaf

Dracaena fragrans

Height: up to 1.5m (5ft)

Spread: up to 75cm (30in)

MADAGASCAR DRAGON TREE
Dracaena marginata
This dragon tree has the same care requirements. It's narrow, so good if you're short on space.

SONG OF INDIA
Dracaena reflexa
Another dragon tree with the same needs. Its lush, palm-like leaves are arranged in a spiral around the main stem.

LUCKY BAMBOO

Dracaena sanderiana

Popularly used in feng shui, this plant is often sold with twisted stems. It can be grown in compost or water.

ııı

HOW **NOT** TO KILL IT

LOCATION
Keep the plant at 16–24°C (60–75°F), and no colder than 10°C (50°F) in winter. Avoid draughty spots or places with large temperature fluctuations.

LIGHT
Place it in a bright spot, away from direct sunlight.

WATERING + FEEDING
Use distilled, filtered, or rainwater as the plant is sensitive to the chemicals in tap water. If growing in compost, water when the compost has become slightly dry to the touch. Reduce watering in winter. Feed once in spring and once in summer. Plants growing in water should be given a weak feed every couple of months.

CARE
If the plant is being grown in compost, repot it every 2 years. If growing in water, the water needs a depth of at least 5cm (2in) – make sure the roots are covered. Refresh with tepid water every week.

BROWN LEAF TIPS?
In both plants growing in compost and water, this may be due to chemicals in tap water or because the room is too dry.
💗 **SAVE IT** *Use distilled, filtered, or rainwater. If you think low humidity may be to blame, mist the leaves every couple of days.*

ALGAE IN THE WATER?
This will only affect plants grown in water, and is caused by chemicals in tap water, or by too much light.
💗 **SAVE IT** *Clean the container and pebbles. You might want to switch to an opaque container, and fill it with distilled, filtered, or rainwater. Move your plant away from direct sunlight.*

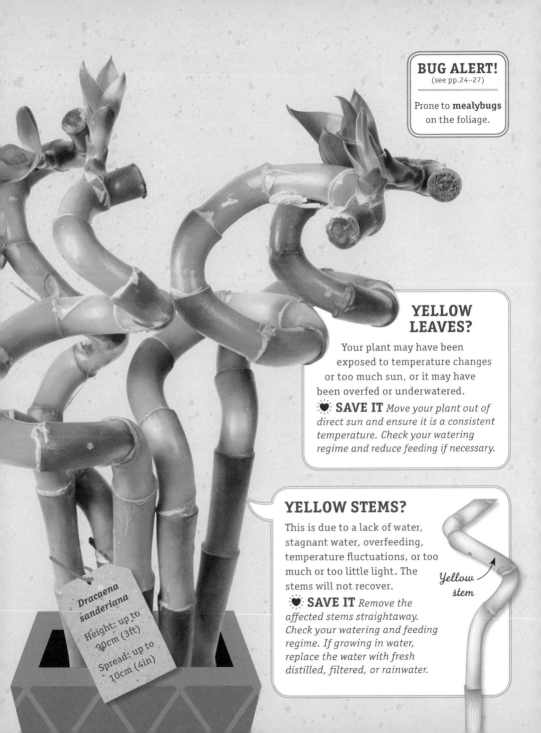

BUG ALERT!
(see pp.24–27)

Prone to **mealybugs** on the foliage.

YELLOW LEAVES?

Your plant may have been exposed to temperature changes or too much sun, or it may have been overfed or underwatered.

☀ **SAVE IT** *Move your plant out of direct sun and ensure it is a consistent temperature. Check your watering regime and reduce feeding if necessary.*

YELLOW STEMS?

This is due to a lack of water, stagnant water, overfeeding, temperature fluctuations, or too much or too little light. The stems will not recover.

Yellow stem

☀ **SAVE IT** *Remove the affected stems straightaway. Check your watering and feeding regime. If growing in water, replace the water with fresh distilled, filtered, or rainwater.*

Dracaena sanderiana

Height: up to 90cm (3ft)

Spread: up to 10cm (4in)

HEN & CHICKS

Echeveria

There are many varieties of this succulent, all producing tiny flowers on tall stems.

‖‖‖

HOW **NOT** TO KILL IT

✓ LOCATION
Keep the plant at 10–24°C (50–75°F). It can tolerate lower temperatures if the compost isn't wet.

LIGHT
Provide lots of bright light. The plant can take some direct sunlight, as long as it is acclimatized gradually.

 WATERING + FEEDING
From spring to autumn, water when the top 2–3cm (1in) of compost is dry. Water sparingly in winter. Feed once a month in spring and summer.

CARE
Top the compost with a layer of gravel – this will keep the neck of the plant dry and will show off the whole plant nicely. Don't choose too large a pot as it will do better if a little cramped. Add some horticultural grit to the compost when planting to improve drainage. Baby plants need more care than large, established ones. Plants will enjoy a holiday outside in summer.

DRY, CRISPY LEAVES AT THE BASE?

This is just a case of the older leaves dying off. It is normal and nothing to worry about.

☀ **SAVE IT** *Gently pull the dead leaves away.*

BLEACHED OR BROWN PATCHES ON LEAVES?

This may be sunburn, or rot from where water droplets have gathered on the leaves.

☀ **SAVE IT** *Move your plant out of direct sunlight. Don't splash the leaves – water from below if necessary (see Water it, pp.18–19).*

BUG ALERT!
(see pp.24–27)

Prone to **mealybugs** on the foliage, and, if the plant has been outside in summer, **vine weevil** grubs in the compost.

YELLOW, TRANSLUCENT, OR SOGGY LEAVES?

This is most likely a sign of overwatering, and, if not dealt with, can lead to the plant rotting.

☀️❤️ **SAVE IT** *Reduce watering and check that the compost and pot are well drained.*

LEAVES SHRIVELLING?

Your plant needs water.

☀️❤️ **SAVE IT** *Water your plant lightly over a few days – the leaves should soon become plump again.*

AEONIUM
Aeonium
Care for these rosette-forming succulents in the same way as hen & chicks. They come in a wide range of colours.

TIGER JAWS
Faucaria
Care for this succulent in the same way. Don't worry about the spiny-looking edges to the leaves – they're not sharp.

Echeveria secunda var. 'Glauca'

Height & spread: up to 10cm (4in)

POINSETTIA

Euphorbia pulcherrima

The red bracts of poinsettias give them a festive feel. Exposure to cold can kill them, so wrap them up well to take them home.

||||||||||||||||||||||||||||||||||||||||||||||||||||||||||

HOW **NOT** TO KILL IT

✔ **LOCATION**
Keep the plant in a warm, bright spot, away from cold draughts or radiators, in a room that is 15–23°C (65–73°F). Maintain a constant temperature.

LIGHT
Place it in bright light, away from direct sun.

WATERING + FEEDING
Water so that the compost is moist, but not soggy. Allow the top 1–2cm (½–¾in) of compost to dry out before watering again. Let any excess water drain away.

CARE
Humidity will make the bracts last longer, so stand on a pebble-filled tray of water and mist from time to time, especially if the plant is in a centrally heated room.

BUG ALERT!
(see pp.24–27)
Prone to **mealybugs** and **red spider mites** on the foliage.

~ Pale bract

PALE LEAVES AND BRACTS?

This happens naturally with age. It could be that your plant isn't getting enough sunlight or is too hot.

☀ **SAVE IT** *Move your plant to a brighter spot. If in a room warmer than 23°C (73°F), move somewhere cooler. Place it on a pebble-filled tray of water and mist the leaves.*

BROWN TIPS OR EDGES ON LEAVES OR BRACTS?

The air is too dry.

☀ **SAVE IT** *Mist the leaves frequently, especially if the plant is in a centrally heated room.*

YELLOWING, DROPPING LEAVES?

Your plant could be too hot and dry, or it might not be getting enough light or water.

💓 **SAVE IT** *Check your plant isn't near a radiator and has enough bright light. Water the plant if the compost is dry. Raise humidity by placing it on a pebble-filled tray of water and misting the leaves.*

NO MORE BRACTS?

The bracts will fade in spring, but you can try to make your plant reflower the following year.

💓 **SAVE IT** *During mid-spring, prune it back to about 10cm (4in) in height, repot, and water. In summer, keep your plant in a cool spot with bright, indirect light (about 15°C/60°F). In early autumn, put your plant in a cupboard or cover it with a black plastic bag for 14 hours each night for 10 weeks. Don't forget to take it out during the day. It should flower again for the festive season.*

Euphorbia pulcherrima
Height & spread: up to 60cm (24in)

PLANT WILTING AND/OR LOSING ITS LEAVES?

Leaf loss often follows wilting. It could be due to exposure to cold or cold draughts, under- or overwatering, or a sudden change in conditions.

💓 **SAVE IT** *Soak underwatered plants in tepid water for an hour – they should revive quickly. Check overwatered plants for root rot and remove affected areas (see Plant diseases, pp.28–29). Allow the compost to dry out before you water again. Make sure your plant is in a warm spot, free of draughts. Your plant is likely to die if it has been exposed to cold.*

FIDDLE-LEAF FIG

Ficus lyrata

A lush, exotic tree that brings a sense of the jungle to your living room.

IIIIIIIIIIIIIIIIIIIIIIIIIIIIIIIIIIIIII

Whole plant

HOW **NOT** TO KILL IT

LOCATION
Choose a bright spot in a warmish room (18–24°C/64–75°F), away from any radiators or draughts, and no colder than 13°C (55°F) in winter. The plant doesn't like being moved, so once you have found the right spot for it, leave it there.

LIGHT
Place it in bright light, but direct summer sun will burn the leaves.

WATERING + FEEDING
From spring to autumn, water only when the top 2–3cm (1in) of soil is dry. Water sparingly during winter. Feed monthly in spring and summer.

CARE
Clean the leaves if dusty. Mist them occasionally – more in summer, or if the room is centrally heated. You might need to support the plant with a cane. When the plant is young, repot it into a slightly larger pot every spring. As it matures, replace only the top 5cm (2in) of compost.

BUG ALERT!
(see pp.24–27)

Prone to **mealybugs, scale insects**, and **red spider mites** on the foliage.

SUDDEN LEAF LOSS?

A sudden loss of a lot of leaves could be due to your plant being moved, which will cause it stress. Alternatively, it could be caused by dry air, over- or underwatering, over- or underfeeding, temperature, and draughts.

SAVE IT *Avoid moving your plant. If your plant has not recently been moved, check its location and your care regime.*

LEAF TIPS TURNING BROWN?

This is probably due to low humidity, or inadequate or erratic watering.

☀️ **SAVE IT** *Mist the leaves regularly – especially in centrally heated rooms. Make sure you water at regular intervals, and check that the whole root ball gets wet.*

Ficus lyrata

Height: up to 3m (10ft)

Spread: up to 1m (3ft)

Leaf spot

DARK PATCHES OR SPOTS ON LEAVES?

Dark patches could be sunburn. Small dark spots could be leaf spot.

☀️ **SAVE IT** *Move it out of direct sunlight. If leaf spot, remove any affected leaves and treat with fungicide (see Plant diseases, pp.28–29).*

(see Plant diseases, pp.28–29)

SHARE THE CARE

WEEPING FIG
Ficus benjamina
Care for this fig as you would a fiddle-leaf fig – keep it away from draughts and radiators, and try not to move it.

RUBBER PLANT
Ficus elastica
An easy-care alternative to the fiddle-leaf fig. Wipe the leaves frequently and don't overwater.

NERVE PLANT

Fittonia

Found in Peruvian rainforests, this striking plant is grown for its veined leaves. Fittonia verschaffeltii has red veining.

IIIIIIIIIIIIIIIIIIIIIIIIIIIIIIIIIIIIIIIIIIIIIIIIIIIIII

HOW **NOT** TO KILL IT

LOCATION
This plant loves warmth, so put it in a room that is 15–23°C (60–75°F). A spot in a bathroom or kitchen could be ideal if the temperature is consistent. The nerve plant is also well suited to being grown in a terrarium.

LIGHT
Place it in a partially shaded spot as it doesn't like bright sunlight – most windowsills are probably too bright.

WATERING + FEEDING
From spring to autumn, water generously with tepid water when the top 1cm (½in) of compost is dry, ensuring the excess water drains away. Water more sparingly in winter and don't let the plant sit in cold, wet compost.

CARE
Stand the plant on a pebble-filled tray of water and mist the leaves daily to ensure that it has enough humidity.

Fittonia verschaffeltii
Height: up to 15cm (6in)
Spread: indefinite

BUG ALERT!
(see pp.24–27)

Prone to **aphids**.

Aphids on the underside of a young leaf

PLANT HAS COLLAPSED?

Nerve plants are prone to collapsing dramatically if their compost is too dry.

☀ **SAVE IT** *Water well and mist the leaves. Ensure you water your plant correctly (see left). If the compost has been dry for a long time, your plant may not recover.*

LEAF TIPS TURNING BROWN?

This is due to low humidity.

☀ **SAVE IT**
Mist the leaves regularly and stand your plant on a pebble-filled tray of water.

YELLOW LEAVES?

This is probably due to overwatering.

☀ **SAVE IT** *Nerve plants like moisture, but not soggy compost. Remove the yellowed leaves and ensure that you allow the compost to dry out between waterings.*

Yellowing leaves

SHARE THE CARE

VELVET PLANT
Gynura aurantiaca
It's hard to resist stroking this plant's velvety leaves. It has similar needs to a nerve plant, but likes bright light.

POLKA DOT PLANT
Hypoestes
This plant has similar needs, but can take more bright light. It is good for a terrarium.

ENGLISH IVY

Hedera helix

Unlike many houseplants, ivy does best in cool temperatures, so this tough, trailing plant should be used as an attractive addition to a colder room.

HOW **NOT** TO KILL IT

LOCATION
Place it in a cool or even cold room (2–16°C/35–60°F). It should be grown up a pole, planted in a hanging planter, or could be placed in a pot on a shelf. It's good for unheated porches or draughty hallways.

LIGHT
Provide bright but indirect light. Non-variegated types will tolerate lower light levels.

WATERING + FEEDING
From spring to autumn, keep the compost moist, but not wet, watering when the top 2–3cm (1in) of compost is dry. Water more sparingly in winter. Feed monthly in spring and summer.

CARE
Mist the plant on warm days. Repot in spring when the roots have filled the pot.

SPINDLY GROWTH?

The room is too warm, or your plant isn't getting enough light.

💚 **SAVE IT** *Move your plant to a cool, bright spot. Cut off the affected areas to encourage more bushy growth.*

Hedera helix
Height & spread: up to 30cm (1ft)

BROWN LEAF TIPS OR EDGES?

This happens if the air around your plant is too warm and dry.

💖 **SAVE IT** *Mist the leaves, or move your plant to a cooler spot, especially if it is in a centrally heated room or if the weather is warm.*

Dry, brown leaf edges

SPOTTED LAUREL
Aucuba japonica

Care for this evergreen garden shrub in the same way as English ivy. It's great for a cool spot, such as a porch or hallway.

VARIEGATED LEAVES TURNING ALL GREEN?

Your plant isn't getting enough light.

💖 **SAVE IT** *Move it to a brighter spot.*

Leaves have lost variegation

JAPANESE ARALIA
Fatsia japonica

An evergreen garden shrub that can be cared for in the same way as English ivy.

Signs of red spider mites

BUG ALERT!
(see pp.24–27)

Prone to **red spider mites** on the foliage.

AMARYLLIS

Hippeastrum

Often sold in a kit, these bulbs will produce striking flowers year after year with the right care.

HOW **NOT** TO KILL IT

 LOCATION
Keep the planted bulb in a bright spot that's around 20°C (68°F) and away from draughts. Once it's in flower, you could move it to a slightly cooler spot to prolong the flowers.

 LIGHT
Place it in bright light and keep out of direct sun.

 WATERING + FEEDING
Keep the compost moist, but not soggy. Feed once a month.

CARE
Amaryllis is often sold in a planting kit with compost and a pot. Plant the bulb in autumn or winter, ensuring the pot isn't much larger than the bulb. Use multi-purpose compost and add perlite for drainage. Don't bury the whole bulb – the neck and "shoulders" should be above the compost. It should flower 6–8 weeks after planting. Turn the pot regularly to prevent the plant growing towards the light.

BUG ALERT!
(see pp.24–27)

Prone to **mealybugs** on or under the leaves and around the plant.

NO MORE FLOWERS?

Amaryllis flowers will fade in spring, but it is possible to get them to reflower the following winter or spring.

☀ SAVE IT *After flowering, cut off the spent flower spike to about 5cm (2in) above the bulb and feed and water as usual. You could put the plant outside in summer. In early autumn, give the plant a rest period in a room at 10–13°C (50–55°F). Stop feeding and reduce watering during this time. The foliage will die back. After 8–10 weeks of rest, replace the top 5cm (2in) of the compost, bring back into a warm room, and feed and water as before. It should then flower 6–8 weeks later.*

Hippeastrum
Height: up to
60cm (24in)
Spread: up to
30cm (12in)

FLOWER SPIKE
SLOW TO DEVELOP?

You may have the plant in too cool a room.

❤ **SAVE IT** *Move it to a warmer spot (around 20°C/68°F). Check the compost is moist, but not soggy.*

NO FLOWER THE
FOLLOWING WINTER?

This may be because your plant has not rested for long enough in the right conditions.

❤ **SAVE IT** *Ensure the rest period is 8–10 weeks and you are providing enough light and the correct care (see No more flowers?).*

KENTIA PALM

Howea fosteriana

Popular since the 19th century, this low-maintenance palm brings an air of elegance to your home.

||||||||||||||||||||||||||||||||||||||||||||||||||||

HOW **NOT** TO KILL IT

LOCATION
Provide temperatures of 18–24°C (64–75°F), and a minimum temperature of 12°C (54°F) in winter. It needs humidity, and should be kept away from radiators.

LIGHT
Place it in bright but indirect light. Direct sun will scorch the leaves.

WATERING + FEEDING
Water in spring and summer so the compost is moist, but allow it to dry out slightly in between. Reduce watering in winter. Feed monthly in spring and summer.

CARE
Clean the leaves regularly – you could stand it under a tepid shower, or in summer rain. Only repot when roots are visible above the compost or growing through the drainage holes. Mist the leaves regularly to create humidity – more freqently in a hot room.

Whole plant

LEAF TIPS GOING BROWN?

The air could be too dry or too cold. Alternatively, it may have been underwatered.

☀ SAVE IT *If the plant is near a radiator, move it away. Check that the temperature isn't too low and water if the compost is dry. Cut off the brown tips with scissors just inside the brown area.*

BUG ALERT!
(see pp.24–27)

Prone to **scale insects**, **mealybugs**, and **red spider mites** on the foliage.

DULL LEAVES?

A lack of shine on the leaves can be caused by low humidity.

☀ **SAVE IT** *Keep it away from radiators and mist the leaves frequently.*

YELLOWING LEAVES?

Lower leaves can turn yellow with age. If the problem is widespread, this could be a sign of underwatering.

☀ **SAVE IT** *Check your watering regime (see left).*

LEAVES GOING BROWN?

Older, lower leaves will naturally turn brown and die, but check that you haven't overwatered your plant.

☀ **SAVE IT** *Cut any unsightly brown leaves off at the base using secateurs. Check your watering regime (see left).*

Howea fosteriana
Height: up to 3m (10ft)
Spread: up to 80cm (32in)

SHARE THE CARE

PARLOUR PALM
Chamaedorea elegans
An easy-to-grow palm with the same care as Kentia palm. It is quite compact, only reaching about 1m (3ft).

BUTTERFLY PALM
Dypsis lutescens
Another, similar palm with the same care needs. It likes good light and a slightly humid atmosphere.

TOP 5 PLANTS FOR
YOUR BATHROOM

Plants can add a lush, verdant feel to your bathroom. Many plants love the high humidity produced by baths and showers – here are five beautiful specimens to try.

Nerve plant

Fittonia

This rainforest plant has beautiful, veined foliage. It loves high humidity, so is perfect for a bathroom. Keep it in a partially shaded spot.

See Nerve plant, pp.78–79.

Maidenhair fern

Adiantum raddianum

If you take plenty of baths and showers, your maidenhair fern will be happy, as it enjoys a humid atmosphere. It has pleasing, delicate foliage.

See Maidenhair fern, pp.32–33.

Velvet plant
Gynura aurantiaca

This pretty foliage plant has soft, velvety leaves. It will begin to trail once the plant matures. It likes humidity and bright light, so put it within a few feet of a bathroom window.

See Velvet plant, p.79.

Boston fern
Nephrolepis exaltata

The Boston fern thrives in a room with high humidity, making it a good choice for a bathroom. The arching fronds look particularly good in a hanging planter.

See Boston fern, pp.96–97.

Indian rope plant
Hoya carnosa

This climbing plant has beautiful, waxy flowers, and its evening scent is perfect for a relaxing bathtime. It requires lots of light and humidity, so needs to be kept in a bright bathroom.

See Indian rope plant, pp.88–89.

INDIAN ROPE PLANT

Hoya carnosa

This climbing plant has pretty flowers that are especially scented in the evening. 'Variegata' has creamy edges to its leaves.

Whole plant

HOW NOT TO KILL IT

LOCATION
Grow it up a trellis or pole, keeping it at 18–24°C (64–75°F) and above 10°C (50°F) in winter. It can get quite large, so it will need plenty of space.

LIGHT
Place it in a bright spot, out of direct sun, which can scorch the leaves.

WATERING + FEEDING
From spring to autumn, water when the top 2–3cm (1in) of compost dries out, making the compost moist, but not wet. Keep almost dry in winter. Feed monthly from spring to late summer.

CARE
Use well-drained compost. To add humidity, stand the plant on a pebble-filled tray of water. Mist the leaves – more often in a hot room. Don't mist, move, or repot the plant when it is in bud or flower. Remove the top 5cm (2in) of compost and replace with fresh each spring. Only repot if it's completely pot-bound. Don't deadhead the plant or cut off the flowering stalks as these will reflower.

DROPPING FLOWER BUDS?
The compost may be too dry or too wet, or you may have moved or repotted your plant while it was in bud.

💟 **SAVE IT** *Avoid moving your plant while it is in bud or flower. Check your watering regime (see left).*

NO FLOWERS?
Your plant may not be in a bright enough spot – it can survive low light levels but won't flower. You may have removed the flowering stalks.

☀ **SAVE IT** *Move it to a brighter spot. Each stalk can produce flowers for many years, so be sure not to deadhead – let the spent flowers fall off naturally.*

BUG ALERT!
(see pp.24–27)

Prone to **mealybugs, whitefly, scale insects**, and **aphids**.

SHARE THE CARE

MINIATURE WAX PLANT
Hoya bella
This is a more compact plant that has similar care needs to an Indian rope plant, but likes a higher temperature (no less than 16°C/60°F in winter).

DRIPPING FLOWERS?

The flowers produce nectar to attract pollinators – this is normal.

☙ **SAVE IT**
Do nothing!

DROPPING LEAVES, OR BLACKENED LEAVES?

This could be due to overwatering, or excessive cold in winter.

☀ **SAVE IT** *Check that the compost isn't waterlogged. Water more sparingly. Move the plant if it is too cold.*

Blackened leaf

Hoya carnosa 'Variegata'

Height: up to 4m (13ft)

Spread: up to 70cm (28in)

FLAMING KATY

Kalanchoe blossfeldiana

These succulent plants are sold all year round and have long-lasting red, pink, orange, white, or yellow flowers.

HOW **NOT** TO KILL IT

LOCATION
Keep it at 18–24°C (65–75°F), and above 10°C (50°F) in winter.

LIGHT
Place it in bright light, including some direct sun – close to an east- or west-facing window in spring or summer, and a south-facing one in winter.

WATERING + FEEDING
Water when the top 2–3cm (1in) of compost is dry, but more sparingly in winter. Ensure the pot has good drainage so the plant isn't sitting in soggy compost. If you keep the plant after it has flowered, feed it once a month in spring and summer.

CARE
Pinch off the flowers as they fade. After flowering, cut back all the flowered stems. Most people discard their plant after flowering, but it is possible to make it flower again if you follow a specific care regime (see No more flowers?).

NO MORE FLOWERS?

The flowers will fade after around 8 weeks, but you can try to get your plant to flower again.

☀ **SAVE IT** *Put your plant outside in summer, then bring it indoors in autumn as temperatures start to fall. Place in a cool but bright location, stopping feeding, and watering less. It will then need 14 hours of darkness each night for at least a month to reflower - place it in a cupboard every evening if it is in a room with artificial light. Resume feeding and watering around 8 weeks later when the plant forms flower buds.*

BROWN PATCHES ON LEAVES?

This is probably sunburn.

☀ **SAVE IT** *Move your plant so that it receives less direct sunlight.*

Brown patches

LEAVES HAVE A RED EDGE?

This is nothing to worry about – the leaves turn red if they are in the sun.

☀ **SAVE IT** *Your plant is happy, but watch for sunburn on the leaves.*

PLANT WILTING?

Your plant may have got too cold, or it might be over- or underwatered.

♥ **SAVE IT** *Move it to a warmer spot (such as away from a windowsill that gets too cold at night) and out of cold draughts. Check your watering regime (see left).*

SHARE THE CARE

CALANDIVA
Kalanchoe
Calandiva® series
Bears masses of small, rose-like, fully double flowers. Treat in exactly the same way as you would a flaming Katy.

Kalanchoe blossfeldiana
Height: up to 30cm (12in)
Spread: up to 20cm (8in)

STEM TURNED BROWN OR BLACK AND MUSHY?

This is stem rot, due to overwatering.

♥ **SAVE IT** *Remove affected areas of the plant. For more information, see Plant diseases (pp.28–29).*

Black and mushy stem

SENSITIVE PLANT

Mimosa pudica

This plant has a charming party trick – when you touch it, its leaves fold up and its stems droop.

HOW **NOT** TO KILL IT

 LOCATION
Keep it at 18–24°C (64–75°F), and above 15°C (60°F) in winter.

 LIGHT
Provide plenty of bright light, including some direct sun.

 WATERING + FEEDING
Keep the compost moist but not soggy, and just moist in winter. Feed once a month during spring and summer.

CARE
Sensitive plants like humidity, so place the plant on a pebble-filled tray of water. Often sold in a planting kit, they are easy to grow from seed. It will produce pretty, pink flowers in summer.

PLANT REACTS SLOWLY WHEN TOUCHED AND IS SLOW TO RECOVER?

You've been touching it too much, making it less "ticklish". After being touched, the leaves can take up to half an hour to unfold.

☀ **SAVE IT** *Give your plant a break from being touched for a while – it might need several weeks to become sensitized again.*

Leaves when open

Leaves when closed

| **BUG ALERT!** (see pp.24–27) | Prone to **red spider mites** on the foliage. |

Whole plant

PLANT GETTING LARGE AND LEGGY?

This is normal. The plant becomes less attractive over time, and most people discard their plant in autumn, after it has finished flowering.

❤ **SAVE IT** *Cut it back to the desired size, or sow or buy a new plant in spring.*

LEAVES CLOSED BUT THE PLANT HASN'T BEEN TOUCHED?

The plant can react if shaken or brushed by a breeze. The leaves will also fold up naturally at night.

❤ **SAVE IT** *Do nothing!*

LEAVES TURNING YELLOW AND FALLING OFF?

Your plant is probably too cold.

❤ **SAVE IT** *Move it to a warmer spot.*

Mimosa pudica

Height: up to 60cm (2ft)

Spread: up to 30cm (1ft)

SWISS CHEESE PLANT

Monstera deliciosa

A 1970s favourite, the swiss cheese plant is making a comeback. It will instantly give any room a fun, jungle look.

HOW NOT TO KILL IT

LOCATION
It will survive at 10–24°C (50–75°F), but will only grow if over 18°C (65°F). Provide space as it can get pretty large.

LIGHT
Place it in a bright or lightly shaded spot, such as a few feet from a window. Keep out of direct sunlight.

WATERING + FEEDING
Water after the top of the compost has dried out a little. Feed once a month during spring and summer.

CARE
Wipe the leaves occasionally to keep them free of dust, and mist them from time to time. Once the plant reaches 75cm (30in) tall, it will need support, such as a moss pole or bamboo cane. Tuck the long aerial roots into the compost or the pole. Repot every spring when young. When your plant gets too big to repot easily, remove the top 5cm (2in) of compost and replace with fresh.

YELLOW LEAVES?
Overwatering is the most likely cause, especially if the leaves are also wilting. This may have led to root rot. If you've watered your plant correctly, it may need feeding.

💗 **SAVE IT** *Reduce watering if you have overwatered. Feed your plant once a month in spring and summer. Check for root rot, removing any affected roots. For more information, see Plant diseases (pp.28–29).*

LEAF TIPS AND EDGES TURNING BROWN?
This may be due to dry air or compost, low temperatures, or because your plant has become pot-bound.

💗 **SAVE IT** *If your plant is in a warm room (over 24°C/75°F) with dry air, stand it on a pebble-filled tray of water and mist the leaves regularly. If it is near a radiator, move it away. Check the room isn't too cold. Repot if necessary.*

THE PLANT IS "CRYING"?

Water will sometimes drip from the leaves of your plant if the compost is too wet.

❤️ **SAVE IT** *Increase the time between waterings, making sure that you allow the compost to dry out slightly each time.*

BUG ALERT!
(see pp.24–27)

Prone to **mealybugs** on the undersides of the leaves.

UNCUT LEAVES?

Young plants and new stems do not produce cut leaves. Uncut leaves on mature stems are a sign your plant is unhappy.

❤️ **SAVE IT** *If you have a young plant, be patient! If not, ensure your plant is in a good location that is over 18°C (65°F) and you are providing the correct watering, feeding, and care (see left).*

Monstera deliciosa

Height & spread: up to 1.8m (6ft)

SHARE THE CARE

HORSEHEAD PHILODENDRON
Philodendron bipinnatifidum
An impressive plant with the same care needs. Ensure you give it plenty of room.

SWISS CHEESE VINE
Monstera obliqua
With the same care demands as a Swiss cheese plant, this variety has unusual, oval holes in its leaves.

BOSTON FERN

Nephrolepis exaltata 'Bostoniensis'

This graceful fern looks great on a pedestal or in a hanging planter – its broad, arching fronds will hang down below the level of the vase.

ı ı

HOW **NOT** TO KILL IT

LOCATION
The plant will love moisture and humidity – so is a great choice for a bathroom. Keep the room's temperature at 10–21°C (50–70°F).

LIGHT
Provide good, but indirect light, as direct sunlight will burn the leaves.

WATERING + FEEDING
Keep the compost moist (but not wet) at all times. Feed once a month from spring to autumn.

CARE
Stand the plant on a pebble-filled tray of water and mist the leaves every few days in summer, or if the central heating is on. Remove any dead fronds. Repot in spring if the roots have filled the existing pot.

BUG ALERT!
(see pp.24–27)
Prone to **scale insects**, **mealybugs**, and **red spider mites** on the foliage.

PALE FRONDS?

Your plant may need feeding, or it might be in too bright a spot.

♥ **SAVE IT** *Ensure you feed your plant once a month from spring to autumn. Move it to a shadier spot if necessary.*

BROWN FROND TIPS? FRONDS DYING BACK?

Some older fronds will die back naturally. If the problem is widespread, the air is probably too dry, or your plant isn't getting enough water.

♥ **SAVE IT** *Increase the humidity by standing your plant on a pebble-filled tray of water and misting the leaves every few days. Ensure that the compost is moist but not soggy.*

BIRD'S NEST FERN
Asplenium nidus
This fern has similar requirements to a Boston fern, but copes well with lower light levels. Wipe the leaves to keep them shiny.

Nephrolepis exaltata 'Bostoniensis'

Height & spread: up to 75cm (30in)

FRONDS TURNING YELLOW?

The air may be too dry or too warm.

♥ **SAVE IT** *Mist the leaves regularly and reduce the temperature of the room if necessary.*

SILVER LADY
Blechnum gibbum
This large fern has similar needs, but will tolerate dry air and prefers soft water.

DESERT CACTI

Opuntia

The many types of cacti come in a range of shapes. Opuntia is a common genus within the cactus family.

HOW **NOT** TO KILL IT

LOCATION
Put a cactus somewhere warm (13–29°C/55–85°F). In winter, move it to a cooler spot to encourage flowers.

LIGHT
Place it in bright sunlight, but shield it from strong, direct sun in the middle of the day in summer. Provide air circulation on hot days. If moving the plant into direct sunlight, acclimatize it gradually.

WATERING + FEEDING
In spring and summer, keep the compost moist using tepid water. In autumn and winter, keep the compost almost dry. Feed once in spring and again in summer.

CARE
Grow in cactus compost. Wear thorn-proof gloves when handling, or carefully wrap the plant in newspaper.

| BUG ALERT! (see pp.24–27) | Prone to **mealybugs** and **scale insects**. |

SHRIVELLING
This is due to underwatering. Contrary to popular opinion, cacti do need watering!

SAVE IT *Water the compost a small amount every day for the next few days, but don't let the plant sit in wet compost.*

MUSHY PLANT?
The mushy areas of the plant are areas that have rotted. This is due to overwatering, often combined with low temperatures.

SAVE IT *Depending on how far the rot has spread, you could try repotting your plant into fresh cactus compost. Cut away any rotted roots.*

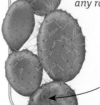

Soft, rotten areas

NO FLOWERS?

It is possible to coax some cacti into flowering (such as mammillaria, opuntia, astrophytum, and rebutia) when they are a few years old.

☀️ **SAVE IT** Stop watering in autumn, then in winter place your plant in a cool, light room, and keep the compost dry. In spring, bring into a warmer spot before resuming gentle watering and feeding. Keeping the plant in a small pot will also encourage it to flower.

BROWN/WHITE DISCOLORATION?

This is sunburn, and occurs if the plant is in very strong sunlight.

☀️ **SAVE IT** *Move your plant out of very strong midday sun in summer.*

CACTUS SPLITTING?

This is due to overwatering.

☀️ **SAVE IT** *Stop watering – the scar should heal over. Check your watering regime (see left). Also check that the compost and pot are well-drained.*

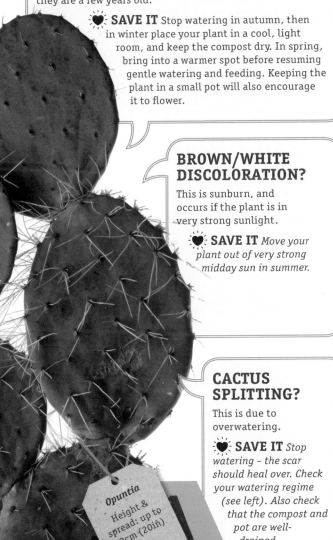

Opuntia
Height & spread: up to 50cm (20in)

MONK'S HOOD
Astrophytum ornatum
This small cactus has a round shape and can produce yellow flowers.

CROWN CACTUS
Rebutia
This popular cactus produces pretty, tubular flowers close to its base.

RADIATOR PLANT

Peperomia metallica

Radiator plants hail from the floors of tropical rainforests. There are many types, grown for their varied and interesting leaves.

HOW **NOT** TO KILL IT

LOCATION
Provide temperatures of 18–25°C (65–77°F) from spring to autumn, and a minimum temperature of 10°C (50°F) in winter.

LIGHT
Place it in a bright or partially shaded spot, out of direct sun – filtered light from an east- or north-facing window is ideal. It will do well under fluorescent light, so is a good choice for an office.

WATERING + FEEDING
Water with tepid water, whenever the compost is beginning to dry out. Water from below to avoid wetting the leaves (see Water it, pp.18–19). In winter, water sparingly. Feed monthly in spring and summer.

CARE
It needs good drainage. Stand it on a pebble-filled tray of water as it will appreciate humidity.

BUG ALERT!
(see pp.24–27)

Prone to **mealybugs** under the leaves and around the plant.

Peperomia metallica
Height & spread: up to 20cm (8in)

— *Corky swellings*

CORKY SWELLINGS UNDER THE LEAVES?

This is oedema, caused by too much watering in winter.

☀ **SAVE IT** *Ensure you water your plant sparingly in winter. For more information, see Plant diseases (pp.28–29).*

LEAF DROP?

This can be caused by a lack of water, or if the plant is too cold.

☀ **SAVE IT** *Water your plant. If it is located in a room cooler than 10°C (50°F), move it to a warmer spot.*

CREEPING BUTTONS
Peperomia rotundifolia
A pretty, trailing peperomia with small, fleshy, button-like leaves. It has the same care needs.

BABY RUBBER PLANT
Peperomia obtusifolia
Care for this upright plant as you would a radiator plant. Its leaves are often splashed with gold, grey, or cream.

PLANT WILTING DESPITE WATERING?

You may have overwatered your plant, causing root rot.

☀ **SAVE IT** *Check your plant for root rot and remove any affected areas. For more information, see Plant diseases (pp.28–29).*

MOTH ORCHID

Phalaenopsis

The orchid family is enormous. Moth orchids are the easiest to grow, and their flowers last for many weeks.

HOW **NOT** TO **KILL IT**

LOCATION
Place the plant in a room with a temperature of around 18–26°C (65–80°F).

LIGHT
Put it in bright, but indirect light – near an east-facing window is ideal.

WATERING + FEEDING
Water by dipping and draining (see Water it, pp.18–19). Do this about once a week in spring and summer, and around every 2 weeks in winter. Ideally, use distilled, filtered, or rainwater. Provide orchid feed once a month during spring and summer, but every 2 months in autumn and winter.

CARE
Grow in orchid compost in a transparent container so that light can reach the roots. Don't cut off or cover the roots that are sticking into the air – they will rot. Once the flowers fade, cut back the flowering stem to a bud lower down, and it should produce a new flower spike within a few months.

BUD DROP

This could be due to under- or overwatering, low humidity, or temperature fluctuation.

☀❤ **SAVE IT** *Water normally (see left), and place your plant on a pebble-filled tray of water. Avoid moving your plant when it is in bud.*

BUG ALERT!
(see pp.24–27)

Prone to **scale insects** and **mealybugs** on the foliage.

Phalaenopsis
Height: up to 1m (3ft)
Spread: up to 30cm (12in)

NO FLOWERS?

It may take several months for your plant to reflower. However, a lack of flowers can also be due to a lack of bright light, over- or underfeeding, or excessive temperature fluctuations. Your plant may need repotting.

♥ **SAVE IT** *Move your plant to a brighter spot, ensuring you feed it monthly in spring and summer and every 2 months in autumn and winter. Repot if necessary. Lower night-time temperatures (13–18°C/55–65°F) can stimulate reflowering, so put it on a windowsill or in a cooler room for a few weeks.*

CHANGE IN LEAF COLOUR?

The leaves should be a grassy green. Yellowing of older leaves is natural, but for younger leaves it can be a sign of too much bright sunlight or underfeeding. The leaves becoming darker can be a sign of a lack of bright sunlight.

Yellow leaves

♥ **SAVE IT** *Adjust your plant's light levels accordingly. If it is spring or summer, ensure you feed your plant once a month.*

Shrivelled leaves

SHRIVELLED LEAVES?

This probably means that not enough water is reaching the leaves. This is often due to underwatering, but can be caused by root damage. Limp leaves could also be a sign there is not enough humidity.

♥ **SAVE IT** *Healthy roots are silvery or green, while brown, mushy roots indicate overwatering and hollow, crispy roots are a sign of underwatering. If roots are damaged, trim off the worst of the damage and repot in fresh compost. Raise the humidity by standing your plant on a pebble-filled tray of water.*

PYGMY DATE PALM

Phoenix roebelenii

A more delicate version of its cousin, the Canary Island date palm (Phoenix canariensis), the pygmy date palm (Phoenix roebelenii) has elegant, arched fronds.

HOW NOT TO KILL IT

LOCATION
The pygmy date palm likes rooms that are around 18°C (65°F) – warmer than many other palms. It grows to around 1.8m (6ft) so needs a fair amount of space.

LIGHT
Place it in bright but indirect light, out of direct sun.

WATERING + FEEDING
Water freely in summer when the top 2–3cm (1in) of compost feels dry. Keep the compost barely moist in winter. Feed it monthly from spring to late summer.

CARE
Stand it on a pebble-filled tray of water to increase humidity around the plant, especially in summer or in a heated room.

BUG ALERT!
(see pp.24–27)
Prone to **scale insects**, **mealybugs**, and **red spider mites** on the foliage.

LEAVES NOT DARK GREEN?
This could be due to underfeeding.

SAVE IT *Feed your plant once a month from spring to late summer.*

LEAF TIPS GOING BROWN?
The air could be too dry. Underwatering or cold air may also be the cause.

SAVE IT *If your plant is standing near a radiator, move it away. Check the temperature isn't too low (less than 10°C/50°F) and water if the compost is dry. Cut off the brown tips with scissors.*

BROWN SPOTS ON THE LEAVES?
This could be caused by overwatering or exposure to cold.

SAVE IT *Remove the affected foliage and check your plant's position and care (see left).*

Phoenix roebelenii

Height & spread: up to 1.8m (6ft)

Brown spots

LEAVES GOING BROWN?

If only the lower leaves are affected, don't worry – it's natural for old leaves to turn brown and die. But check that you haven't overwatered the plant, rotting the roots.

☀ **SAVE IT** *Cut off the unsightly brown leaves at the base using secateurs or scissors. Ensure you are only watering when the top 2–3cm (1in) of the compost is dry. If the problem persists, check for root rot, removing any affected roots. For more information, see Plant diseases (pp.28–29).*

For more information, see Plant diseases (pp.28–29).

SHARE THE CARE

LADY PALM
Rhapsis excelsa
This palm needs similar care to a pygmy date palm, but will tolerate lower light levels.

DWARF FAN PALM
Chamaerops humilis
Provide this slow grower with the same care, but it will tolerate lower temperatures. It will only reach 1.2m (4ft).

TOP 5 PLANTS FOR
LOW LIGHT

All plants need some light in order to grow, but some, especially those with larger leaves, are better at coping with a shadier spot. Here are five shady characters to try.

Bird's nest fern
Asplenium nidus

This easy-care fern has a rosette of lush, shiny leaves. It copes well in low light, but wipe the leaves occasionally to keep them shiny and allow light to get to them.

See Bird's nest fern, p.97.

Peace lily
Spathiphyllum

Peace lilies are forgiving plants with glossy green leaves and striking white flowers. They don't mind low light levels and can also put up with erratic watering.

See Peace lily, pp.124–125.

Heart-leaf philodendron
Philodendron scandens

This philodendron has glossy, heart-shaped leaves. It's a climber, so train it up a mossy pole.

See Heart-leaf philodendron, p.63.

Japanese aralia
Fatsia japonica

This striking plant, with its large, lush, glossy leaves, copes well in low light levels and can survive temperatures as low as 0°C (32°F) in winter.

See Japanese aralia, p.81.

Cast iron plant
Aspidistra eliator

As its name suggests, this plant has a strong constitution. Wipe the leaves to allow maximum light to get to them. It's forgiving of under-watering, but it has one pet hate – very wet compost.

See Cast iron plant, p.125.

MISSIONARY PLANT

Pilea peperomioides

Also known as a Chinese money plant, this sought-after houseplant is grown for its pretty, lily pad-like leaves.

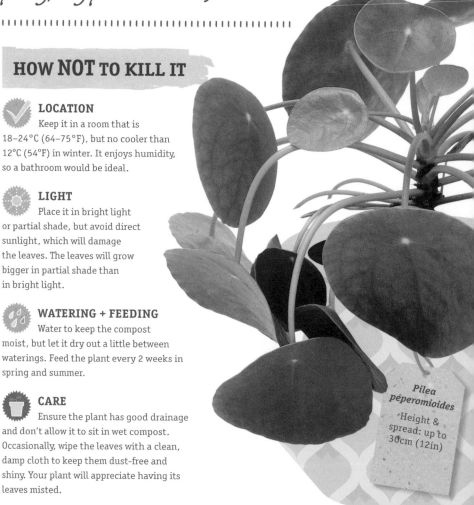

HOW **NOT** TO KILL IT

LOCATION
Keep it in a room that is 18–24°C (64–75°F), but no cooler than 12°C (54°F) in winter. It enjoys humidity, so a bathroom would be ideal.

LIGHT
Place it in bright light or partial shade, but avoid direct sunlight, which will damage the leaves. The leaves will grow bigger in partial shade than in bright light.

WATERING + FEEDING
Water to keep the compost moist, but let it dry out a little between waterings. Feed the plant every 2 weeks in spring and summer.

CARE
Ensure the plant has good drainage and don't allow it to sit in wet compost. Occasionally, wipe the leaves with a clean, damp cloth to keep them dust-free and shiny. Your plant will appreciate having its leaves misted.

Pilea peperomioides
Height & spread: up to 30cm (12in)

LEAVES FACING IN ONE DIRECTION?

The leaves will grow towards the light.

♥ **SAVE IT** *Rotate your plant regularly so that it keeps its mounded shape.*

LEAVES TURNING YELLOW OR DROPPING OFF?

If the leaves are turning yellow at the base of the plant, don't worry – these are just ageing leaves. If the leaves are yellow all over, this could be due to overwatering or underwatering.

♥ **SAVE IT** *Check your watering and care regime (see left).*

POWDERY, WHITE PATCHES ON THE LEAVES?

This is powdery mildew. It won't kill your plant, but it does look unsightly.

♥ **SAVE IT** *Remove the affected leaves promptly. Try to improve the air circulation around your plant. For more information, see Plant diseases (pp.28–29).*

White patches →

SHARE THE CARE

FRIENDSHIP PLANT
Pilea involucrata **'Moon Valley'**
This striking perennial has similar needs to a missionary plant, but likes higher humidity. Try keeping it in a terrarium.

ALUMINIUM PLANT
Pilea cadierei
This plant can be cared for in the same way as a friendship plant, as it also adores high humidity. Mist the leaves often and place on a pebble-filled tray of water.

STAGHORN FERN

Platycerium bifurcatum

These ferns grow like air plants in the wild. At home, they can be grown with or without compost, and are often sold on a mount.

‖‖

HOW **NOT** TO KILL IT

LOCATION
Keep in a humid environment – a bathroom could be ideal. Ensure the temperature is 10–24°C (50–75°F).

LIGHT
Place it in very bright, but indirect light. Direct sunlight will scorch the leaves.

WATERING + FEEDING
Staghorn ferns absorb water through their roots and fronds. Keep the compost lightly moist at all times. To water mounted plants, place them upside down in a bath of tepid water and leave for 20 minutes, or run under tepid tap water. Drip dry before re-hanging. Water weekly if in a hot, dry room, every 2–3 weeks if it is cool or humid. Feed monthly in spring and summer.

CARE
Mist your plant regularly with tepid water, especially if it is in a hot, dry room.

> **BUG ALERT!**
> (see pp.24–27)
>
> Prone to **scale insects** on the undersides of the leaves.

Platycerium bifurcatum
Height & spread: up to 1m (3ft)

FROND TIPS BROWNING OR WILTING?

Your plant is not getting enough water.

❤ **SAVE IT** *Water your plant more often and increase humidity by misting the leaves more frequently.*

PLANT WATERED BUT STILL WILTING?

It may have root rot.

❤ **SAVE IT** *Check your plant for root rot and remove any black and mushy roots. For more information, see Plant diseases (pp.28–29).*

REGAL ELKHORN FERN
Platycerium grande
With pale green, antler-like fronds, this houseplant is larger than the staghorn fern but you can care for it in the same way.

ANTLER FRONDS BROWNING OR BLACKENING AT THE BASE?

This is due to overwatering.

❤ **SAVE IT** *Don't water your plant for a few weeks, then return to a normal watering regime.*

Antler fronds come from the centre

Shield fronds surround the edge

BROWN SHIELD FRONDS?

Staghorn ferns have small fronds at their base. These are "shield" fronds and help to take up water and protect the roots. They naturally turn brown with age.

❤ **SAVE IT** *Don't do anything – it's a normal process for the lower fronds to turn brown. Don't remove them.*

AFRICAN VIOLET

Saintpaulia

These popular, furry-leaved plants have flowers in a wide range of colours. Their small size makes them ideal if you are short on space.

||||||||||||||||||||||||||||||||||||||||||||||||||||||||||||||||||||||||||||||

HOW NOT TO KILL IT

LOCATION
Provide warmth (16–23°C/ 60–73°F) and high humidity. A bathroom or kitchen windowsill is ideal, as long as it isn't too cold.

LIGHT
Place it in bright, indirect light. Shade from direct sunlight, which will scorch the leaves.

WATERING + FEEDING
Water when the top 2–3cm (1in) of compost has dried out. The plant should be watered from below for about 30 minutes (see Water it, pp.20–21). This avoids wetting the leaves. Feed once a month from spring to late summer.

CARE
Stand the plant on a pebble-filled tray of water to provide humidity. Cut off any spent flowers. African violets grow best in small pots, so don't repot too often.

YELLOW LEAVES?
This could be due to dry air, too much sun, or poor watering or feeding.

❤ **SAVE IT** *Move your plant out of direct sunlight. Raise humidity and check your feeding and watering regime (see left).*

NO FLOWERS?
African violets often stop blooming in winter, due to lower light levels. In spring to autumn, a lack of flowers could be due to a care issue.

❤ **SAVE IT** *In winter, move your plant to a bright, south- or west-facing window. If it is spring to autumn, check that you are feeding your plant correctly, and that it is in a warm enough location.*

BUG ALERT!
(see pp.24–27)

Prone to **mealybugs** on the undersides of the foliage.

BROWN SPOTS ON LEAVES?

This can happen if the leaves are splashed with water, or your plant is watered with cold water.

☀ **SAVE IT** *Always water from below to prevent the leaves being splashed. Stand your plant in a saucer of water for about 30 minutes. Use water that is at room temperature.*

Brown spots ⟵

Saintpaulia
'Bright Eyes'

Height & spread: up to 15cm (6in)

PLANT WILTING?

This is a result of over- or underwatering.

☀ **SAVE IT** *Ensure you are watering your plant from the bottom when the top 2–3cm (1in) of compost has dried out. Check for crown or root rot (see Plant diseases, pp.28–29).*

GREY FLUFF ON LEAVES?

This is probably a grey mould called botrytis.

☀ **SAVE IT** *Remove affected areas and treat with fungicide. For more information, see Plant diseases (pp.28–29).*

Grey fluff

SNAKE PLANT

Sansevieria trifasciata

This striking plant with stiff, sword-like leaves is virtually indestructible – the only way to kill it is through overwatering and cold temperatures.

HOW NOT TO KILL IT

LOCATION
A snake plant isn't at all fussy about its location. It will thrive at 10–26°C (50–80°F), and doesn't mind draughts or dry air.

LIGHT
Ideally, provide bright, indirect light, though it will tolerate some direct sun. It will also cope in low light levels, but the variegated leaves may revert to all-green.

WATERING + FEEDING
Water moderately in spring and summer, and sparingly during autumn and winter. Feed once a month in spring and summer.

CARE
Grow in a heavy pot to prevent the plant toppling. Be careful not to damage the leaf tips – this will stop the plant growing. Wipe the leaves occasionally to keep them shiny. Only repot if pot-bound.

LEAVES FALLING SIDEWAYS?

You may have under- or overwatered your plant, or it isn't getting enough light. It may also be pot-bound. Tall, older leaves do sometimes collapse.

SAVE IT *Check your care regime and light levels (see left). Repot if necessary.*

YELLOWING LEAVES?

This is usually caused by overwatering, especially during winter. Check the base and roots of your plant for rot.

SAVE IT *Allow the compost to dry out. Consider moving your plant to a warmer spot if temperatures are low. Check for root rot, removing any affected roots. For more information, see Plant diseases (pp.28–29).*

Yellow leaf

WRINKLED LEAVES?

If the leaves on your plant are wrinkled, you have probably underwatered it.

☀ **SAVE IT** *Water your plant lightly over a few days and the leaves should firm up again.*

Wrinkled leaf

BUG ALERT!
(see pp.24–27)

Prone to **mealybugs** on the foliage.

Sansevieria trifasciata

Height: up to 1.2m (4ft)

Spread: up to 50cm (20in)

SHARE THE CARE

AFRICAN SPEAR
Sansevieria cylindrica
An African spear has the same care needs as a snake plant. Its cylindrical leaves are often braided.

AFRICAN MILK BUSH
Euphorbia trigona
This striking succulent has sharp thorns and the same care requirements.

CREEPING SAXIFRAGE

Saxifraga stolonifera

This attractive, trailing plant has pretty, veined leaves that have reddish undersides.

IIIIIIIIIIIIIIIIIIIIIIIIIIIIIIIIIIIIIIII

Brown patches

HOW NOT TO KILL IT

 LOCATION
Place it in a cool to moderate room (10–21°C/50–70°F), that is no colder than 7°C (45°F) in winter. It looks great in a hanging planter or on a shelf – the runners (trailing stems) can reach 75cm (30in).

LIGHT
Provide bright, but indirect light, avoiding direct sunlight.

WATERING + FEEDING
Water freely from spring to autumn, whenever the top 2–3cm (1in) of compost dries out. Water from below. This avoids splashing water on the leaves or the base of the stems, which can cause fungal disease. Reduce watering during winter. Feed monthly in spring and summer.

CARE
The plant will enjoy some humidity if your home is warm, so place it on a pebble-filled tray of water. It will grow fast and doesn't like to be pot-bound, so you will probably need to repot it every year.

BROWN PATCHES ON LEAVES?
This is sunburn.
💓 **SAVE IT** *Move your plant out of direct sun.*

PLANT WILTING?
This may be due to overwatering, especially in winter.
💓 **SAVE IT** *Check the compost. If it's soggy, allow the compost to dry out. You might want to check the roots for root rot – affected roots will be dark and mushy. Try cutting off these areas and repotting into fresh compost. For more information, see Plant diseases (pp.28–29).*

| **BUG ALERT!** (see pp.24–27) | Prone to **red spider mites** on the foliage and **aphids** around the plant. |

SWEDISH IVY

Plectranthus

This plant needs similar care to a creeping saxifrage, but is more tolerant of dry air. It's a good plant for a hanging planter.

Saxifraga stolonifera

Height & spread: up to 20cm (8in)

RUNNERS TURNING BROWN?

This is due to a lack of water or humidity.

☀ **SAVE IT** *Check your watering regime and stand the plant on a pebble-filled tray of water. Mist the leaves regularly.*

UMBRELLA TREE

Schefflera arboricola

This leafy foliage plant has an exotic air and is easy to grow. You can keep it at the desired height by cutting off the top.

HOW **NOT** TO KILL IT

LOCATION
Place it in a reasonably warm room (13–24°C/55–75°F). Ensure it doesn't fall below 13°C (55°F) in winter.

LIGHT
Provide bright, indirect light.

WATERING + FEEDING
From spring to autumn, water when the top 2–3cm (1in) of compost has become dry. It doesn't mind a bit of underwatering but won't be happy if you overwater it, as this can lead to root rot (see Plant diseases, pp.28–29). Reduce watering in winter. Feed once a month in spring and summer.

CARE
You could mist the leaves in warm weather or if the plant is in a warm room. Wipe the leaves with a clean, damp cloth from time to time to keep them free of dust.

STICKY LEAVES?

Umbrella trees are particularly prone to scale insects – the first sign is sticky leaves, which eventually turn black and sooty. You will also see brown bumps underneath the leaves.

SAVE IT *Rub off the insects and wipe the leaves clean, removing any sooty mould. Treat the leaves with insecticide. For more information, see Plant pests (pp.24–27).*

LEAVES FALLING OFF?

This could be due to temperature fluctuations or your plant may be in too dark a spot. You may have over- or underwatered.

SAVE IT *Check that your plant is in a warm enough spot (13–24°C/55–75°F) and has plenty of indirect light. Keep it away from cold draughts. Check your watering regime (see left).*

PLANT LEANING TO ONE SIDE?

It is leaning towards the light.

☀ **SAVE IT** *Turn the plant regularly or tie it to a bamboo cane or moss pole.*

BUG ALERT!
(see pp.24–27)

Prone to **scale insects** and **red spider mites** on the foliage.

DROOPING LEAVES?

This is due to overwatering or underwatering.

☀ **SAVE IT** *Check the compost. If it's soggy, allow it to dry out and check for signs of root rot (see Plant diseases, pp.28–29). Ensure you water when the top 2–3cm (1in) of compost has dried out.*

Schefflera arboricola

Height: up to 1.4m (5ft)

Spread: up to 1m (3ft)

SHARE THE CARE

CROTON
Codiaeum variegatum
A croton requires similar care to an umbrella tree, but needs a slightly warmer room (at least 15°C/60°F in winter), likes humidity, and should be protected from fluctuating temperatures.

ZEBRA PLANT
Aphelandra squarrosa
Often sold in flower, a zebra plant needs similar care, but must be kept above 15°C (60°F) in winter. Overwatering will cause the lower leaves to drop.

CHRISTMAS CACTUS

Schlumbergera buckleyi

Christmas cacti are forest cacti – jungle evergreens rather than desert natives. They bear flowers in winter.

HOW **NOT** TO KILL IT

✓ LOCATION
Place it in a room that's 18–24°C (65–75°F). To ensure it flowers, rest twice a year in cooler temperatures (see No flowers?).

LIGHT
Provide bright, indirect light.

WATERING + FEEDING
Water when the top 2–3cm (1in) of compost is dry, letting any excess water drain away – don't let the plant sit in soggy soil. Water more sparingly in winter. Feed monthly in spring and summer.

CARE
Place the plant on a pebble-filled tray of water for humidity, misting the leaves twice a week when it's not in flower. Repot into a slightly larger pot every 1–2 years when the root ball has filled the pot (it likes to be snug). Add some grit to the compost.

> **BUG ALERT!**
> (see pp.24–27)
>
> Prone to **mealybugs** in the nooks and crannies of stems.

NO FLOWERS?

Your plant will need a rest period in order to flower again.

❤ **SAVE IT** *After flowering, place your plant in a cool, unheated room (about 12°C/55°F) for an 8-week rest period, and water less. Put it outside in summer in a shady spot, and water and feed as normal. In autumn, give your plant a second rest period in a cool, unheated room, ideally where no lights will be switched on at night, for 8 weeks. Then return it to its flowering position and care for as normal.*

LEAVES TURNING RED?

This is a sign that your plant is getting too much sunlight.

💗 **SAVE IT** *Move it out of direct sun.*

Reddish leaves

Schlumbergera Hybrid
Height & spread: up to 35cm (14in)

BUDS DROPPING?

This can be caused by moving your plant when in bud, incorrect watering, or fluctuating temperatures.

💗 **SAVE IT** *Move your plant from its rest position to its regular position when in early bud, then don't move it again. Check your watering regime (see left).*

SHARE THE CARE

EASTER CACTUS
Schlumbergera gaetneri
This species flowers in spring. Like a Christmas cactus, it likes a spell outside in summer, followed by a rest period to encourage reflowering.

MISTLETOE CACTUS
Rhipsalis baccifera
With the same care needs, this succulent is great for a hanging planter. Mature plants may produce fruit.

BABY'S TEARS

Soleirolia soleirolii

Baby's tears has a spreading mat of tiny leaves that spill over the edge of a pot. Forms with variegated or golden leaves are also available.

HOW **NOT** TO KILL IT

✔ LOCATION
It is comfortable in temperatures from 10–21°C (50–70°F), but it will be happiest at the cooler end of this range.

☀ LIGHT
Place it in bright, indirect light.

💧 WATERING + FEEDING
Keep the compost moist, but not soggy from spring to autumn, and just moist in winter. Feed once during spring and once during summer.

🪴 CARE
Stand the plant on a pebble-filled tray of water to provide humidity, especially in a warm room. Trim into shape with scissors. Baby's tears is sometimes recommended for terrariums, but be warned: it has a tendency to take over.

BROWN FOLIAGE?

Either your plant isn't getting enough water, the air is too dry or hot, or it has been scorched by the sun.

☀ **SAVE IT** *Keep the soil moist from spring to autumn, and just moist in winter. Raise the humidity by standing your plant on a pebble-filled tray of water. Ensure it is not in direct sunlight.*

PLANT WILTING?

This may be due to over- or underwatering.

☀ SAVE IT *Ensure you're keeping the compost moist from spring to autumn, and just moist in winter – it should never be soggy. Check the roots for root rot, removing any affected areas. For more information, see Plant diseases (pp.28-29).*

PIGGYBACK PLANT
Tolmiea menziesii
Care for this plant as you would baby's tears. It produces tiny plants on top of its mature leaves.

Soleirolia soleirolii
Height: up to 10cm (4in)
Spread: indefinite

LEGGY PLANT?

Your plant may become leggy if the temperature is too high.

☀ SAVE IT *Move to a cooler spot – 10–16°C (50–60°F) is ideal.*

BEAD PLANT
Nertera granadensis
With similar needs to baby's tears, this likes plenty of light and doesn't mind cool rooms. Don't let it dry out.

PEACE LILY

Spathiphyllum

With glossy, green leaves and occasional white flowers, this is a forgiving plant that is good for beginners.

HOW **NOT** TO KILL IT

 LOCATION
Provide a warm room with a temperature of 13–26°C (55–80°F). Keep the plant away from cold draughts.

LIGHT
Place it in bright, indirect light.

WATERING + FEEDING
Water when the top 2–3cm (1in) of compost has become dry. Feed monthly from spring to late summer. You may need to use distilled, filtered, or rainwater if you live in an area that has hard water.

CARE
Place the plant on a pebble-filled tray of water. You could also mist the leaves once or twice a week, especially if the plant is in a warm room. Snip off any fading flowers and yellowing leaves. Repot the plant each year in spring.

BUG ALERT!
(see pp.24–27)
Prone to **mealybugs** on the undersides of the foliage.

WHOLE PLANT DROOPING?

Your plant needs water.

💗 **SAVE IT** *Plunge your plant into a bucket of water for half an hour or so and allow it to drain – it should recover quickly (see Water it, pp.18–19).*

YELLOW LEAVES?

Old leaves yellow naturally. Yellowing younger leaves are a sign of stress.

💗 **SAVE IT**
Check your plant is in a good location and you are watering and feeding it correctly (see left). Repot if the root ball has filled the pot. Try switching to distilled, filtered, or rainwater.

BROWN PATCHES ON LEAVES?

This is leaf scorch.

☀ SAVE IT
Move your plant out of direct sunlight to a shadier position.

brown patches

CHINESE EVERGREEN
Aglaonema
This plant has similar care needs as a peace lily, but can tolerate shade and temperature change – great for a hallway.

BROWN LEAF TIPS?

This could be due to lack of humidity, or erratic watering and feeding. It could also be due to hard water.

☀ SAVE IT
Increase humidity around the plant and ensure you are feeding and watering it correctly (see left). Try switching to distilled, filtered, or rainwater.

CAST IRON PLANT
Aspidistra eliator
Has similar care needs. Wipe the leaves occasionally, and only repot if absolutely necessary. It hates wet soil.

Spathiphyllum
Height & spread: up to 60cm (24in)

TOP 5 PLANTS FOR
YOUR LIVING ROOM

Don't relegate houseplants to a dusty corner of your living room – bring them to the fore and grow them in containers that complement your space. Here are five great plants to consider.

Snake plant
Sansevieria trifasciata

This low-maintenance favourite has a strong, architectural look that will allow it to stand out in any room. It is also a great air purifier.

See Snake plant, pp.114–115.

Fiddle leaf fig
Ficus lyrata

This sought-after plant is a favourite with interior designers and has lush, paddle-like leaves. Don't move it after you've found the perfect spot for it, as it has a tendency to drop its leaves if moved.

See Fiddle-leaf fig, pp.76–77.

ZZ plant
Zamioculcas zamiifolia

This striking plant with its lush foliage can really create a point of interest in a room. It doesn't take up much space and is easy to grow.

See ZZ plant, pp.138–139.

Kentia palm
Howea fosteriana

This easygoing palm will bring an air of elegance to your living room. Given good light (but avoiding direct sun) it will grow green and lush. Wipe and mist the leaves occasionally.

See page Kentia palm, pp.84–85.

Swiss cheese plant
Monstera deliciosa

This Seventies favourite is back in fashion and is a great statement plant. Give it a bright or lightly shaded spot and plenty of space – it can grow quite large.

See Swiss cheese plant, pp.88–89.

BIRD OF PARADISE

Strelitzia reginae

It's easy to see how this stunning plant gets its name – the blue and orange flowers look like the head of an exotic, crested bird.

HOW **NOT** TO KILL IT

LOCATION
Provide warmth (at least 20°C/68°F) and humidity. A bright bathroom or conservatory can be ideal. It also likes good air circulation, so you could put it outside in summer. It needs a minimum of around 10°C (50°F) in winter.

LIGHT
Place in as much light as possible, but keep out of direct summer sun.

WATERING + FEEDING
Water freely when the surface of the compost feels dry but don't let the compost become soggy. Water sparingly in winter. Feed monthly in spring and summer.

CARE
Stand on a pebble-filled tray of water and mist the leaves from time to time to increase humidity. Don't repot until the roots are visible at the top of the compost or are growing out of the drainage holes. Wipe the leaves with a clean, damp cloth to keep them dust-free.

NO FLOWERS?

Your plant won't flower unless it is mature (at least 4 years old), and is given light and plant food. It will do best if slightly pot-bound.

SAVE IT *Check your plant has enough light and is adequately fed. It also likes to be snug in its container, so check the plant isn't in too large a pot.*

BROWN LEAVES OR LEAF TIPS AND EDGES?

There might not be enough humidity in the room, or your plant may be underwatered or overfed.

SAVE IT *Check that there is enough humidity and that the plant has been watered and fed correctly (see left).*

BUG ALERT!
(see pp.24–27)

Prone to **scale insects, mealybugs**, and **red spider mites** on the foliage.

YELLOW LEAVES?

This is normal on the lower leaves of the plant – they will eventually drop off. Yellow leaves elsewhere on your plant may be due to under- or overwatering, or there's some aspect of its location that the plant doesn't like.

☀ **SAVE IT** *Gently pull away the yellowed leaves. Check your watering regime and that the plant has enough light and warmth (at least 20°C/68°F).*

ROTTING AT THE BASE?

This is root or stem rot, caused by the compost being too wet.

☀ **SAVE IT** *Try repotting into fresh compost. Ensure that the pot drains well. Don't overwater. For more information, see Plant diseases (pp.28–29).*

Strelitzia reginae
Height: up to 1.8m (6ft)
Spread: up to 75cm (30in)

CAPE PRIMROSE

Streptocarpus

Cape primrose is a charming houseplant that has fresh, green leaves and pretty flowers in a range of colours.

BUG ALERT!
(see pp.24–27)

Look for **mealybugs** on the undersides of the leaves.

HOW NOT TO KILL IT

LOCATION
Place in a bright room. It likes a moderate temperature of 13–21°C (55–70°F).

LIGHT
Provide indirect light. An east- or west-facing window is ideal. Keep the plant out of direct sunlight during summer.

WATERING + FEEDING
Water whenever the top 4–5cm (2in) of compost feels dry – aim to make the compost moist, not wet, and let any excess drain away. Reduce watering in winter. Feed every 2 weeks in spring and summer – a high-potash feed (or specialist streptocarpus feed) will encourage flowers.

CARE
Repot every year in spring, into a slightly larger, shallow pot. Cut off the spent flowers to keep the blooms coming. In autumn and winter, the ends of the leaves die back. This is nothing to worry about – just snip the ends off.

BROWN MARKS ON THE LEAVES?

The leaves could be scorched or splashed with water.

SAVE IT *Move your plant out of direct sunlight. Take care not to wet the leaves when watering your plant.*

Scorch marks

LEAVES ROTTING AT THE BASE?

This may be due to overwatering, your plant sitting in water, or poor drainage.

SAVE IT *Remove any affected leaves and allow the compost to dry out. Check the pot is draining excess water. Let the compost dry out between waterings.*

GREY MOULD ON LEAVES?

This is a plant disease called botrytis.

❤ **SAVE IT** *Remove affected areas and treat with fungicide. For more information, see Plant diseases (pp. 28–29).*

WILTING PLANT?

This is either due to over- or underwatering.

❤ **SAVE IT** *If you think you might have overwatered your plant, leave the compost to dry out – it needs to dry out between waterings. If you think you have underwatered it, water your plant.*

SHARE THE CARE

GLOXINIA
Sinningia speciosa

Gloxinia has similar needs to cape primrose. Place in a bright room and keep away from draughts. It can reflower – wait for it to die back before removing any yellowed stems or leaves, and reduce watering. In spring, repot and resume watering. However, people often discard after flowering.

Streptocarpus
Height: up to 30cm (12in)
Spread: up to 45cm (18in)

LARGE LEAVES BUT FEW FLOWERS?

Your plant has been fed incorrectly, or is not getting enough bright light.

❤ **SAVE IT** *Ensure you feed your plant every 2 weeks in spring and summer, using the correct feed. If it's in a gloomy place, move your plant to a spot with brighter, indirect light.*

AIR PLANTS

Tillandsia

In the wild, these intriguing plants grow attached to other plants. Grow them without compost at home, such as nestled in a glass globe or on a piece of driftwood.

!!

HOW NOT TO KILL IT

LOCATION
A bright kitchen or bathroom can be good as an air plant likes high humidity. Don't let it get too cold (below 10°C/50°F), or expose it to draughts, especially if it is damp from watering.

LIGHT
Provide bright, indirect light. Avoid sunny windowsills as the plant may be burnt by summer sun, and get too cold in winter.

WATERING + FEEDING
Water the plant by dipping and draining (see Water it, pp.18–19). Soak it for 30 minutes, or up to 2 hours if underwatered. Water about once a week in summer or if your home is heated. Use distilled, filtered, or rainwater. You can also water by misting thoroughly several times a week. Once a month, add a quarter dose of plant food to the water. Feed all year round.

CARE
After watering, shake your plant lightly and let it dry upside down for around 4 hours before returning it to its position.

NO FLOWERS?
It can take years for your air plant to be mature enough to flower.

SAVE IT *Do nothing! Some plants turn red before flowering. After it has flowered, your plant will produce "pups" (new plants at the base) and the parent plant will die.*

SOFT BROWN AREAS OR PLANT FALLING APART?
A build up of water between the leaves has lead to rot.

SAVE IT *It's too late to save your plant. Next time, shake the plant lightly after watering and allow to drain upside down.*

CURLING LEAVES OR CRISPY LEAF-TIPS?
They are not getting enough water.

SAVE IT *Water and mist your plant more regularly.*

Crispy leaf-tips

Tillandsia melanocrater tricolor

Height & spread: up to 30cm (1ft)

Tillandsia tectorum

Height & spread: up to 30cm (1ft)

Tillandsia juncea

Height & spread: up to 30cm (1ft)

Tillandsia aeranthos

Height & spread: up to 30cm (1ft)

SHEDDING LEAVES?

It's normal for plants to shed some of their outer leaves. If lots of leaves are being lost, this is a sign that something is wrong with your plant's environment.

☀❤ **SAVE IT** *Gently pull away the outer leaves. Check the light, humidity, and temperature levels around your plant are correct (see left).*

INCH PLANT

Tradescantia zebrina

These unfussy, variegated plants are very easy to care for and look great in a hanging planter.

HOW **NOT** TO KILL IT

LOCATION
Place the plant in a room that is 12–24°C (54–75°F).

LIGHT
Provide bright, indirect light. It can take some direct sun.

WATERING + FEEDING
Water freely when the top 2–3cm (1in) of compost dries out; don't allow it to get waterlogged. Feed once a month during spring and summer.

CARE
Remove any shoots that have plain, green leaves; these grow more strongly than variegated leaves and are less attractive.

BUG ALERT!
(see pp.24–27)

Prone to **aphids** and **red spider mites** on the foliage.

UNVARIEGATED LEAVES?

Your plant is not getting enough sunlight.

❤ **SAVE IT** *Remove the unvariegated leaves and move your plant to a brighter spot.*

LIMP STEMS?

The stems trail naturally, but if they look especially limp, this is probably due to underwatering or root rot, which is caused by overwatering.

❤ **SAVE IT** *Ensure you only allow the top 2–3cm (1in) of compost to dry out between waterings. Check for root rot (see Plant diseases, pp.28–29).*

FLAME NETTLE
Solenostemon

Flame nettle, with its bright leaves, is easy to grow and has the same needs as an inch plant. If it becomes leggy, take stem cuttings.

Tradescantia zebrina
Height: up to 15cm (6in)
Spread: up to 20cm (8in)

BROWN LEAF TIPS?

The air is too dry, or your plant is suffering from a lack of water.

❤ **SAVE IT** *Mist the leaves every 3–4 days. Check that you're giving your plant enough water.*

SPINDLY GROWTH OR LOSING LOWER LEAVES?

This could be due to too little light, not enough water, or not enough feed. However, it's more likely that your plant is a few years old – inch plants become spindly with age, shedding their lower leaves.

❤ **SAVE IT** *Check your care regime (see left). If your plant is old and past its best, try taking stem cuttings and potting them up to make fresh plants.*

YUCCA

Yucca elephantipes

With its spiky leaves and trunk-like stems, this shrub brings a touch of the exotic to your home.

IIIIIIIIIIIIIIIIIIIIIIIIIIIIIIIIIIIIIIIIIIIIIIII

Whole plant

BUG ALERT!
(see pp.24–27)

Prone to **scale insects** and **mealybugs** on the foliage.

HOW NOT TO KILL IT

LOCATION
Provide temperatures of 7–24°C (45–75°F), but not lower. A yucca is not fussy – it can tolerate fluctuations in temperature and doesn't mind dry air. Keep the plant away from children, though, as the leaves have sharp ends.

LIGHT
Place it in bright light; it can even take some direct sun. If moving your plant into direct sunlight, acclimatize it gradually.

WATERING + FEEDING
Water moderately from spring to autumn, whenever the top 5cm (2in) of compost has dried out. Water more sparingly in winter. Feed it every 2 months in spring and summer.

CARE
Wipe the leaves occasionally with a clean, damp cloth to keep them shiny and free of dust.

BENDING LEAVES?
This could be due to under- or overwatering, or some kind of shock to your plant, such as moving or repotting it.

SAVE IT *Check you allow the top 5cm (2in) of soil to dry out between waterings, and water more sparingly in winter. If you need to move your plant, move it gradually towards the new position over a week to allow it to acclimatize.*

BROWN OR BLACK SPOTS ON THE FOLIAGE?
This is leaf spot, caused by bacteria or fungi.

SAVE IT *Remove any affected leaves and treat with fungicide. For more information see Plant diseases (pp.28–29).*

Black spots

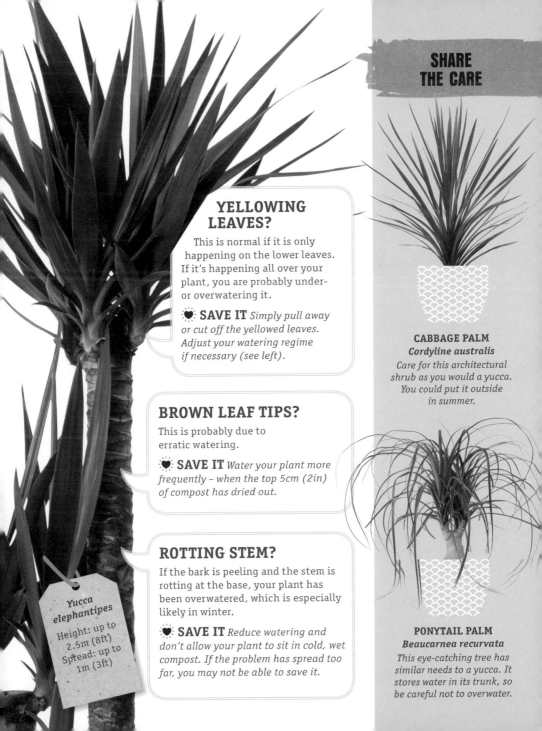

YELLOWING LEAVES?

This is normal if it is only happening on the lower leaves. If it's happening all over your plant, you are probably under- or overwatering it.

❤ **SAVE IT** *Simply pull away or cut off the yellowed leaves. Adjust your watering regime if necessary (see left).*

BROWN LEAF TIPS?

This is probably due to erratic watering.

❤ **SAVE IT** *Water your plant more frequently – when the top 5cm (2in) of compost has dried out.*

ROTTING STEM?

If the bark is peeling and the stem is rotting at the base, your plant has been overwatered, which is especially likely in winter.

❤ **SAVE IT** *Reduce watering and don't allow your plant to sit in cold, wet compost. If the problem has spread too far, you may not be able to save it.*

Yucca elephantipes
Height: up to 2.5m (8ft)
Spread: up to 1m (3ft)

SHARE THE CARE

CABBAGE PALM
Cordyline australis
Care for this architectural shrub as you would a yucca. You could put it outside in summer.

PONYTAIL PALM
Beaucarnea recurvata
This eye-catching tree has similar needs to a yucca. It stores water in its trunk, so be careful not to overwater.

ZZ PLANT

Zamioculcas zamiifolia

This striking, upright plant is easy to grow and doesn't mind being underwatered.

HOW **NOT** TO KILL IT

✓ LOCATION
Keep the plant in a warm room (15–24°C/60–75°F), all year round. It will tolerate dry air.

LIGHT
For a lush plant, place it in bright light, out of direct sun. However, it will tolerate lower light levels.

WATERING + FEEDING
Water so that the compost is just moist and allow the top 5cm (2in) to dry out between waterings, all year round. Don't let the plant sit in wet compost. Feed once a month from spring to late summer.

CARE
Wipe the leaves with a clean, damp cloth to keep them looking shiny and to allow enough light to reach them.

> **BUG ALERT!**
> (see pp.24–27)
> Prone to **mealybugs** and **red spider mites** on the foliage.

YELLOWING LEAVES?

Your plant has been overwatered, or is sitting in wet compost. This can lead to root rot.

☀ **SAVE IT** *Allow the compost to dry out. If the plant looks very sickly, check for signs of root rot - brown, mushy roots. Remove any affected areas and repot. For more information, see Plant diseases (pp.28–29).*

MANY DROPPING LEAVES?

You may have shocked your plant by moving it, perhaps from a shaded to sunny spot. Alternatively, it may be too dry or too wet at the roots.

☀ **SAVE IT** *Acclimatize your plant gradually to a new position. Check whether the compost is too dry or too wet, adjusting your watering regime accordingly.*

BROWN PATCHES ON LEAVES?

This is sunburn.

☀ SAVE IT
Move your plant out of direct sunlight.

Brown patches

Zamioculcas zamiifolia

Height: up to 1m (3ft)
Spread: up to 60cm (2ft)

SHARE THE CARE

SAGO PALM
Cycas revoluta
This ancient plant has been around since the dinosaur era. Care for it in the same way as a ZZ plant.

GUIANA CHESTNUT
Pachira aquatica
This plant is often sold with a braided trunk and has similar care needs to the ZZ plant.

INDOOR BONSAI

Various

Bonsai are young trees trained to look like mature trees in miniature. The bonsai featured here, Chinese elm, is one of many trees you can buy grown like this.

HOW **NOT** TO KILL IT

✔ LOCATION
In the growing season, keep the tree at 15–21°C (60–70°F). Move it to a cooler spot during winter (at least 10°C/50°F). Avoid placing in draughts or near radiators.

LIGHT
Place it in bright light, but avoid direct summer sun.

WATERING + FEEDING
In a shallow tray, the compost can dry out quickly. Keep the compost moist, but not wet. Ideally, use rainwater. Provide with bonsai feed once a month from spring to mid-autumn.

CARE
Grow in a specialist bonsai mix. Stand the tree on a pebble-filled tray of water and mist the leaves for humidity. Repot in spring if the roots have filled the pot. Place the tree outside in the summer.

SPINDLY GROWTH, PALE LEAVES?

Your tree may not be getting enough light, especially in winter.

♥ **SAVE IT** *Move it to a brighter spot. Specialist growers use grow lights in winter to boost light levels.*

CRISPY LEAVES?

Dry, crispy leaves are a sign of underwatering.

♥ **SAVE IT** *Check your watering regime.*

BUG ALERT!
(see pp.24–27)

Prone to **scale insects, mealybugs, powdery mildew, aphids, vine weevils,** and **red spider mites.**

YELLOW LEAVES?

The leaves of deciduous bonsai turn yellow before falling in autumn. In other seasons, or on evergreen bonsai, yellow leaves could be due to over- or underwatering or incorrect feeding, temperatures, or light levels. These can also occur after repotting.

❤ SAVE IT *Ensure the compost is kept moist, not wet and check for root rot (see Plant diseases, pp.28–29). Check you are giving your plant the right care.*

TREE LOSING LEAVES?

Deciduous bonsai drop their leaves in autumn. Some leaf-loss may also occur in spring. Leaf-loss in other seasons or in evergreen trees can be caused by a change in conditions (such as repotting) or incorrect care.

❤ SAVE IT *Check the location is suitable, and that you are providing the correct care (see left).*

CRISPY LEAVES? BLACK OR BROWN TIPS ON LEAVES?

Dry, crispy leaves are a sign of underwatering. Dark leaf-tips are due to overwatering or cold.

❤ SAVE IT *Move your tree to a warmer spot and check your watering regime.*

Ulmus parvifolia

Height & spread: up to 50cm (20in)

TREE BECOMING LEGGY OR LOSING SHAPE?

Your bonsai will need to be pruned and trained in order to manage its size and shape.

❤ SAVE IT *Remove one third of the roots each time you repot your bonsai. Pinch or prune out the growing tips and trim new shoots back to one or two sets of leaves in the growing season. Use bonsai wire to train the branches.*

INDEX

ABOUT THE AUTHOR

Veronica Peerless is a gardening writer and editor, both online and in print. She is Contributing Editor at gardenersworld.com and was previously Deputy Editor at *Which? Gardening* magazine. She contributes to several gardening and lifestyle magazines, including *The English Garden* magazine and the *Garden Design Journal*. Veronica acted as a horticultural consultant on DK's *The Gardener's Year*, a role in which she both shaped and wrote content for the book.

ACKNOWLEDGMENTS

Author: Many thanks to Christian King for his support and endless cups of tea while I was writing this book.

Publisher: DK would like to thank Jane Simmonds for proofreading and Vanessa Bird for creating the index. We'd also like to thank houseofplants.co.uk for allowing us to take photos of their plants – African spear, blushing philodendron, butterfly palm, croton, Easter cactus, fiddle-leaf fig, Guinea chestnut, guzmania, hare's foot fern, horsehead philodendron, Indian rope plant, kentia palm, lucky bamboo, mistletoe cactus, parlour palm, snake plant, song of India, ZZ plant, and several other plants that didn't make the final version of the book. The photo of the Calandiva was taken by Katherine Scheele Photography.

Picture credits: The publisher would like to thank the following for their kind permission to reproduce their photographs:

(Key: a-above; b-below/bottom; c-centre; f-far; l-left; r-right; t-top)

5 Garden World Images: Nicholas Appleby (clb). 10 Alamy Stock Photo: blickwinkel / fotototo (cla). 43 Garden World Images: Nicholas Appleby. 116-117 Alamy Stock Photo: blickwinkel / fotototo

All other images © Dorling Kindersley

For further information see:
www.dkimages.com

TOXICITY

Some houseplants are toxic to humans and pets, and can be hazardous if they are ingested, or come into contact with the skin or eyes. For information about which plants are toxic, please visit:

www.rhs.org.uk
www.aspca.org